MANCHESTER CITY CHAMPIONS

1967/68

WE ARE THE

CHAMPIONS!

**MANCHESTER CITY'S
OWN STORY**

– By Joe and Malcolm
and the Players

MANCHESTER CITY CHAMPIONS
1967/68

PHIL GOLDSTONE & DAVID SAFFER

TEMPUS

Dedication

Phil Goldstone: To my late father, Norman Goldstone, who introduced me to the trials and tribulations of being a true Blue. To Marcia, for putting up with me all these years, and to younger son Johnny for helping with the research.

David Saffer: To Leon Phillips, who experienced the Blues' glory years, and Adam, who dreams of witnessing a trophy-winning Blues team.

First published 2005

Tempus Publishing Limited
The Mill, Brimscombe Port,
Stroud, Gloucestershire, GL5 2QG
www.tempus-publishing.com

British Library Cataloguing in Publication Data.
A catalogue record for this book is available from the British Library.

ISBN 0 7524 3611 2

Typesetting and origination by Tempus Publishing Limited.
Printed in Great Britain.

Acknowledgements

We would like to thank the following individuals and organisations for their help with this publication: Francis Lee, Mike Summerbee and Holly Bennion at Tempus Publishing Ltd.

Sincere thanks also to the *Manchester Evening News* for supplying images in this book. Every attempt has been made to acknowledge the original source for copyright of all pictures in this book, but if anyone has any questions relating to this matter they should contact the publishers.

Foreword by Francis Lee

When I joined Manchester City in October 1967, I did so in the belief that the men who brought me to the club, Joe Mercer and Malcolm Allison, were developing a trophy-winning team. Little did I know that the coming three seasons would be the most prolific in the club's history, with City winning the First Division Championship, FA Cup, League Cup, European Cup-Winners' Cup and Charity Shield – an amazing haul of silverware.

The squad assembled by Joe and Malcolm was relatively unknown and inexperienced at the beginning of the 1967/68 campaign and both Joe and Malcolm had themselves been plucked from football's scrapheap by City chairman Albert Alexander. Joe had been out of the game for a year, having left Aston Villa because of poor health, and Malcolm had been dismissed from his job as Plymouth Argyle manager. Mr Alexander hoped his 'dream team' could revive the fortunes of one of English football's best-loved club's.

Guided by Joe and Malcolm, we surprised our rivals by staying the course to clinch one of the most remarkable title races of all time. During a momentous season there were many memorable performances, most notably a 4-1 victory on a snowbound pitch against Tottenham Hotspur, a 3-1 win at Manchester United and our thrilling final game at St James's Park when we beat Newcastle United 4-3 to take the championship trophy back to Maine Road and our ecstatic supporters.

City's class of '68 instantly became household names. Goalkeeper Ken Mulhearn had been recruited from Stockport County; Glyn Pardoe had graduated through the youth ranks along with his cousin Alan Oakes, who would go on to appear in 668 games for City; skipper Tony Book had arrived from Plymouth Argyle in 1966 and was the only player to appear in every game of our championship-winning season; George Heslop had come from Everton and he partnered Mike Doyle, another player from the junior ranks, in the heart of defence.

Regarding the front men, Mike Summerbee had arrived as an unknown from Swindon; Colin Bell had made the short journey from Bury; Neil Young was yet another junior graduate and Tony Coleman had joined from Doncaster Rovers. I was fortunate to complete a strike force that had pace, power, a cutting edge and skill aplenty.

The First Division Championship is the ultimate domestic honour every professional footballe craves and, for the first time, this book tells the story game by game. It was a season to remember fo all the players and everyone connected with the club. The memories linger on even though it wa thirty-seven years ago.

I hope you enjoy reading about the team's escapades in a season when our faithful fans at the en could justifiably claim to be supporting the Football League Champions.

1967/68 First Division Fixtures

19 August	Manchester City v. Liverpool
23 August	Southampton v. Manchester City
26 August	Stoke City v. Manchester City
30 August	Manchester City v. Southampton
2 September	Manchester City v. Nottingham Forest
6 September	Manchester City v. Newcastle United
9 September	Coventry City v. Manchester City
16 September	Manchester City v. Sheffield United
23 September	Arsenal v. Manchester City
30 September	Manchester City v. Manchester United
7 October	Sunderland v. Manchester City
14 October	Manchester City v. Wolverhampton Wanderers
21 October	Fulham v. Manchester City
28 October	Manchester City v. Leeds United
4 November	Everton v. Manchester City
11 November	Manchester City v. Leicester City
18 November	West Ham United v. Manchester City
25 November	Manchester City v. Burnley
2 December	Sheffield Wednesday v. Manchester City
9 December	Manchester City v. Tottenham Hotspur
16 December	Liverpool v. Manchester City
23 December	Manchester City v. Stoke City
26 December	West Bromwich Albion v. Manchester City
30 December	Manchester City v. West Bromwich Albion
6 January	Nottingham Forest v. Manchester City
20 January	Sheffield United v. Manchester City
3 February	Manchester City v. Arsenal
24 February	Manchester City v. Sunderland
2 March	Burnley v. Manchester City
9 March	Manchester City v. Coventry City

16 March	Manchester City *v.* Fulham
23 March	Leeds United *v.* Manchester City
27 March	Manchester United *v.* Manchester City
6 April	Leicester City *v.* Manchester City
12 April	Manchester City *v.* Chelsea
13 April	Manchester City *v.* West Ham United
16 April	Chelsea *v.* Manchester City
20 April	Wolverhampton Wanderers *v.* Manchester City
25 April	Manchester City *v.* Sheffield Wednesday
29 April	Manchester City *v.* Everton
4 May	Tottenham Hotspur *v.* Manchester City
11 May	Newcastle United *v.* Manchester City

Introduction

Formed in 1880 as St Mark's of West Gorton, bankruptcy led to the formation of Manchester City Football Club in 1894. During a topsy-turvy history, City claimed the Second Division Championship four times and the FA Cup twice before clinching the First Division crown under manager Wilf Wild in 1936/37. Second Division Champions and FA Cup winners under Les McDowall following the Second World War, George Poyser took the helm after relegation in May 1963 but resigned at Easter 1965. The last home game of that season, against Charlton Athletic, attracted an attendance of just 8,409 as City finished the 1964/65 Second Division campaign in mid-table.

To the surprise of football pundits, chairman Albert Alexander appointed former England, Arsenal and Everton wing half Joe Mercer in July 1965. Mercer, manager at Sheffield United and Aston Villa, needed a dynamic coach and right-hand man; recruiting former West Ham defender and Plymouth Argyle manager Malcolm Allison, the start of the Blues' golden era began.

In their first season at the helm, City claimed the Second Division title. Adding Tony Book to a nucleus of players including Colin Bell, Tony Coleman, David Connor, Harry Dowd, Mick Doyle, George Heslop, Alan Oakes, Glyn Pardoe, Mike Summerbee and Neil Young, City consolidated their place in top-flight football in 1966/67. When the Blues opened the 1967/68 campaign with a draw against Liverpool at Maine Road followed by two defeats, there was nothing to suggest a title challenge but, with the addition of Francis Lee and Ken Mulhearn, City went head-to-head with Manchester United, Leeds United and Liverpool.

Dazzling performances included victories over Sheffield United, Leicester City, Tottenham Hotspur and Manchester United before City clinched the title over their Old Trafford neighbours with four consecutive wins during the run-in, culminating in a remarkable 4-3 victory at Newcastle United on the season's last day. City used twenty-one players to secure the title. Bell, Book, Coleman, Doyle, Heslop, Lee, Mulhearn, Oakes, Pardoe, Summerbee and Young all made more than thirty appearances. Skipper Book was the only ever-present; top scorer was Young. All are legends.

By the conclusion of the 1969/70 campaign, the dream-team managerial partnership had guided City to FA Cup, League Cup, European Cup-Winners' Cup, and Charity Shield success. It is a remarkable story and this book, containing match reports of every game, statistics and numerous illustrations, comprehensively recalls the players' exploits in City's greatest ever League campaign when they claimed the ultimate honour in English football for the second time.

As an exciting era beckons under Stuart Pearce, turn the clock back thirty-seven years to a time when Manchester City ruled English football. Enjoy the memories.

Phil Goldstone and David Saffer, 2005

Roll of Honour

Football League First Division Champions: 1937, 1968

Football League Second Division Champions: 1899, 1903, 1910, 1928, 1947, 1966

Promotion to the First Division/Premiership: 1951, 1985, 1989, 2000

Division One play-off winners: 1999

European Cup-Winners' Cup: 1970

FA Cup: 1904, 1934, 1956, 1969

Football League Cup: 1970, 1976

FA Charity Shield: 1937, 1968, 1972

FA Youth Challenge Cup: 1986

Pre-Season

Although not among the favourites for the First Division crown, Manchester City had consolidated their place in top-flight football since winning the Second Division title in 1965/66. Manager Joe Mercer was building a squad that many pundits considered capable of winning honours and City were viewed as catching up fast their esteemed neighbours and rivals at Old Trafford. Both Mercer and assistant Malcolm Allison were well aware that the team needed strengthening, especially in attack, but refused to be rushed into panic signings.

Following a 2-0 win at Portsmouth during the close season, City impressed on a tour of West Germany and Belgium with wins over Eintracht Braunschweig and Standard Liege before a resounding 4-1 victory over Borussia Dortmand at Maine Road.

Off the field, to forge better links with supporters, City published a club magazine. *The Official Magazine of Manchester City* included features on players and management, stars of the future, contenders for the championship, new teams to the First Division, the European scene and a brand new competition exclusive to City fans called 'Scoreboard Scoop'.

Joe Mercer penned an article entitled 'Now City Will Become Even Better'. He noted:

A lot of people, and not all of them Manchester City supporters, are pondering what the future holds for us. Pondering if, in fact, we are going to prove a surprise packet in the First Division this season.

I know that many good judges in the game believe Manchester City may well be on the verge of a breakthrough; a breakthrough which can land some honour, whether it be in the league or the cup, on the Maine Road sideboard at the end of the season.

Let me say straightaway that we at Maine Road agree with those judges who say we could be going places. But we would not be so foolish as to substitute the definite for the possible. Looking back, we are certain we have made progress, the record books show that we won promotion. Looking forward, we have high hopes.

It was great when, in May last year, City did go back into the First Division, and as Second Division champions. We knew then that we still needed players, that money was still tight; but we felt we could make one or two judicious buys, and consolidate our status. We did that.

This, as it were, is a half-term report, really. We have gone up, we have stayed up. BUT IT IS NOT ENOUGH. We know the fans think this, and we agree with them.

Mountains were made to be scaled; honours were made to the won. We want to add to the honours list. We intend to do so and we believe we can. But there is no rigid timetable. That way, you will find only dissolution, if things do not work out.

What we do say is that we have spent money wisely and we intend to go on doing that. We have also begun to fashion a type of team new to Maine Road.

PRE-SEASON

Dream team: Malcolm Allison and Joe Mercer.

Emerging is a City team, a method team, if you like, which is abreast of the times, which slots into the present pattern of football. I want all my team to be attackers, when the occasion demands; I want them all going into the tackle, when defence is the order of the day.

There is a difference between league and cup, for instance. My players know they are good cup fighters, just as they know they are good horses for courses, home or away, when it comes to the derby game against Manchester United.

What we have done, what we are doing, is to harness the talent we have to the tactics with which they can produce the best results.

So where are we going? In a word... FORWARD. We are still ready to buy, and we shall do, if we feel we shall get value for money. This season we look forward to an all-round improvement because, for one thing, the players know they are good enough for the First Division.

We do not promise honours, but we would not be surprised if we did land something. Frankly, we figure our chances are better in cup than in league, but even if we don't win anything, of one thing we are sure, and that is that City is going FORWARD. Progress is inevitable because we are laying sure foundations.

That's why we say to our fans: Stick with us, even if it means being patient a little longer. You'll get your shout, all right... and it may come sooner than anyone thinks.

With the club on and off the field moving in the right direction, Joe Mercer's charges were set for a season to remember.

Manchester City v. Liverpool

Football League First Division   **Date:** 19 August 1967   **Referee:** K. Walker (Maidstone)
Location: Maine Road, Manchester   **Attendance:** 49,343

A penalty miss by new City skipper Tony Book was the major talking point of this keenly contested draw to open the new First Division campaign. Book, who succeeded Middlesbrough-bound Johnny Crossan as club captain, had the opportunity to claim the spoils when Liverpool skipper Ron Yeats upended Neil Young on seventy-three minutes, but City's leader blazed a gilt-edged opportunity wide. City could hardly have received a much tougher test than hosting Liverpool, a task made harder when transfer-seeking Alan Ogley was called in as a late replacement after regular 'keeper Harry Dowd dislocated a finger in training.

Ugly crowd scenes were the backdrop as the two teams ran out in front of nearly 50,000 supporters. However, the Blues started confidently and could have opened the scoring in a rip-roaring fifteen minutes when they dominated play.

The visitors battled away and gradually took control, pressurising the hard-working City defence. Book and George Heslop kept Liverpool at bay, while the courageous Ogley pulled off a string of superb saves. The best chance of the half fell to Liverpool striker Tony Hateley just before the interval, when he ran onto a misplaced Glyn Pardoe header, but Book made a miraculous goal-line clearance, heading the ball over the bar.

The second half saw Liverpool in the ascendancy, but they were fortunate not to fall behind when Young's left-foot strike hit the foot of the post, with 'keeper Tommy Lawrence beaten. Roger Hunt thought he had grabbed the lead in the fifty-fourth minute when he had the ball in the net, but the former England striker's effort was ruled offside.

Despite not creating clear-cut chances, City should have claimed two points when Yeats tripped Young. Book's subsequent miss was his only error in an otherwise faultless display.

Heslop took the Man of the Match honours and, after this resolute defensive display, it is clear that City will be a difficult side to beat.

Manchester City 0   **Liverpool 0**

MANCHESTER CITY v. LIVERPOOL

Tony Book challenges Peter Thompson for the ball. Book later missed a penalty.

Manchester City: Ogley, Book, Pardoe, Connor, Heslop, Oakes, Summerbee, Bell, Young, Jones, Coleman

Liverpool: Lawrence, Lawler, Byrne, Smith, Yeats, Hughes, Callaghan, Hunt, Hateley, St John, Thompson

CITY

VERSUS

LIVERPOOL

SEASON
1967-68

MANCHESTER CITY F.C.
MAINE ROAD, MANCHESTER.
LEAGUE DIVISION 1 CHAMPIONSHIP.

SATURDAY, 19th AUGUST 1967
Kick-off 3.0 p.m.

OFFICIAL PROGRAMME

1/-

SOUTHAMPTON v. MANCHESTER CITY

Football League First Division   **Date:** 23 August 1967   **Referee:** R. Paine (Hounslow)
Location: The Dell, Southampton   **Attendance:** 23,675

Disastrous defending by the Blues handed a win to Southampton – in a game that was City's for the taking. Ron Davies proved the match-winner with a late strike after City missed a catalogue of chances.

The clash at the Dell took place amid rumours sweeping Manchester that City had made a firm bid for Bolton striker Francis Lee. As for Mike Summerbee's transfer request, the latest information coming out of Maine Road was that club officials had refused.

Following on from City's gallant draw against Liverpool at the weekend, Joe Mercer made one change for the season's first away game, Mike Doyle replacing John Clay in attack. His decision paid dividends in the opening exchanges, when Tony Coleman gave the visitors the perfect start with an opening goal on three minutes. Saints, looking to bounce back from a 3-0 defeat at Newcastle United, had centre forward Davies in imperious form, to such an extent that City's George Heslop was given the runaround.

Defensive blunders by the Blues gifted goals to Southampton as City, normally so reliable defensively, caved in. With Heslop out of sorts, Davies headed powerfully home before strike partner

Martin Chivers notched a second to put his team ahead for the first time. The goal sparked City into action, and they duly got back into the game after the half-time break when Colin Bell equalised on fifty-two minutes. With everything to play for, both sides went for the win. Coleman worked tirelessly to spark City's fitful attack but without reward. Nevertheless, City looked good for a point until Davies had the last word with a neat finish to secure the points.

Although still early days, it was noted that City could not afford to gift points to their opponents if they were to challenge at the top of the table. Boss Mercer would doubtless have taken note of his side's defensive vulnerability.

Tony Coleman scored City's first goal of the season.

Southampton 3   **Manchester City 2**
Davies (2)   Coleman
Chivers   Bell

SOUTHAMPTON *v.* MANCHESTER CITY

Stalwart in defence Alan Oakes.

Southampton: Forsyth, Webb, Hollywood, Fisher, Gabriel, Walker, Paine, Chivers, Davies, Melia, Sydenham

Manchester City: Ogley, Book, Pardoe, Connor, Heslop, Oakes, Bell, Summerbee, Young, Doyle, Coleman

MANCHESTER C.

MATCH No. 1

CLUB HONOURS

FOUNDED 1885

F.A. Cup Semi Finalists 1897-8 1907-8 1924-5 1926-7 1962-3
F.A. Cup Finalists 1899-1900 1901-2
League Division 3 Winners 1921-2 1959-60
League Division 2 Runners-up 1965-6

THE OFFICIAL PROGRAMME
of the
SOUTHAMPTON FOOTBALL CLUB
AND THE OFFICIAL JOURNAL OF THE FOOTBALL LEAGUE

Price
NINEPENCE

STOKE CITY v. MANCHESTER CITY

ootball League First Division   **Date:** 26 August 1967   **Referee:** D. Brady (Gloucester)

ocation: Victoria Ground, Stoke   **Attendance:** 22,456

he Blues were left still looking for a first win of the season following a three-goal drubbing at the 'ictoria Ground. Despite a sterling performance between the sticks from a fit-again Harry Dowd, nree second-half goals sealed Stoke City's win and it would have been a rout but for Dowd's lazzling display. City looked to bounce back from a 3-2 midweek defeat at Southampton, while .toke aimed for a second home win in four days following a 2-1 victory over Sheffield United.

There was no sign of the shape of things to come in an opening half when City had several opportunities to score. Stroking the ball about and playing attractive football, Mike Summerbee and :olin Bell both looked dangerous when in possession. However Stoke should have edged ahead, so many were their chances.

In the second half, City's vulnerability in central defence began to show, with George Heslop in particular, for a second successive game, having a torrid time. Unable to shackle stand-in striker :alvin Palmer, Stoke's playmaker George Eastham was controlling play. A goal seemed inevitable und it duly arrived in the fifty-third minute when Alan Bloor headed home Mike Bernard's pinpoint cross past an overworked Dowd.

City soon found themselves two behind when Calvin Palmer headed in a left-wing cross from ohn Mahoney past a static defence. Twenty minutes from time, Stoke completed an impressive victory when Harry Burrows hammered in a penalty after Tony Book was penalised for handball.

The danger signs were beginning to flash ominously for the Maine Road club after a second uccessive defeat. One point from 3 games, 6 goals conceded and only 2 scored was not the start ans expected. With no bite in front of goal, little midfield creativity and a clear vulnerability in the heart of defence, Joe Mercer had much to ponder if City, twenty-first in the table, were to get their eason rolling. Not only was his side in need of a striker and a midfield general but, judging by this nept display, it looked like a central defender might also be necessary.

Stoke City 3   Manchester City 0

  Bloor

  Palmer

  Burrows (pen)

STOKE CITY *v.* MANCHESTER CITY

Top form: Harry Dowd.

Stoke City: Banks, Skeels, Bentley, Bloor, Setters, Allen, Bernard, Eastham, Palmer, Mahoney, Burrows

Manchester City: Dowd, Book, Pardoe, Cheetham, Heslop, Oakes, Summerbee, Bell, Doyle, Connor, Young

STOKE CITY

OFFICIAL PROGRAMME

STOKE CITY

v

MANCHESTER CITY

at Victoria Ground, Saturday 26th August, 1967

KICK-OFF 3-15 p.m.   PRICE 6d

MANCHESTER CITY v. SOUTHAMPTON

Football League First Division **Date:** 30 August 1967   **Referee:** K. Wynn (Wolverhampton)
Location: Maine Road, Manchester   **Attendance:** 22,002

City finally got their First Division campaign off the mark with an exhilarating second-half display that yielded three goals in a thrilling victory. A brace apiece from Colin Bell and Neil Young earned a 4-2 win as the Blues moved up to seventeenth in the table. Now City fans would be hoping their team could build on this triumph.

Branded 'disgraceful' by coach Malcom Allison following an inept 3-0 defeat at Stoke City on Saturday, the Blues returned to action in determined mood. Eighth-placed Saints came into the match with some confidence, following a 4-0 romp against West Brom in their last outing.

Joe Mercer brought Paul Hince in for a second start of the season, switched Summerbee to centre forward and Young inside, while a fit-again Tony Coleman returned to the left wing after missing the debacle at Stoke. With Saints strikers Ron Davies and Martin Chivers looking dangerous and full of running, City's beleaguered defence struggled to cope initially and were fortunate to concede only

Roy Cheetham.

two goals. However, after getting back to 2-1 behind at half-time, thanks to a Young strike, Mercer's team came out for the second half a different side.

Full of pace, guile, enthusiasm and endeavour, Mike Summerbee's power, mobility and imagination as leader of the line inspired Bell and Young to show the true quality of their finishing, while Hince gave a convincing display on the right flank. Saints held on until seventy minutes but could do nothing to stop Summerbee setting up Young for the Blues' equaliser. On fire, Hince whipped over a fierce cross for Bell to nod City into the lead before Alan Oakes powered forward to set up a fourth City goal for Bell.

This was an impressive and morale-boosting victory, but Mercer and Allison would have been aware that City still required reinforcements if they were going to progress.

Manchester City 4	Southampton 2
Young (2)	Chivers
Bell (2)	Davies

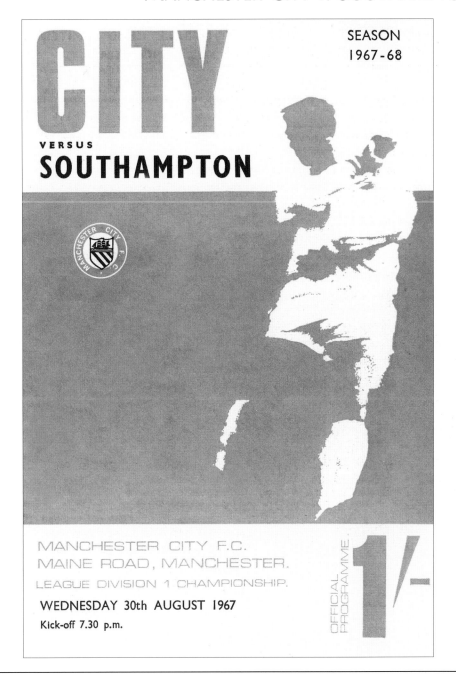

Manchester City: Dowd, Book, Pardoe, Cheetham (Doyle), Heslop, Oakes, Hince, Bell, Summerbee, Young, Coleman

Southampton: Forsyth, Webb, Hollywood, Fisher, Gabriel, Walker, Paine, Chivers, Davies, Melia, Sydenham

MANCHESTER CITY v. NOTTINGHAM FOREST

Football League First Division   **Date:** 2 September 1967   **Referee:** P. Baldwin (Middlesbrough
Location: Maine Road, Manchester   **Attendance:** 29,889

First-half strikes by Mike Summerbee and Tony Coleman sealed a dazzling Blues performance again:
high-flying Nottingham Forest. Joe Mercer's fast-improving side came to the game determined t
prove their 4-2 win against Southampton was no 'flash in the pan', while Forest had won comfortabl
3-1 at Coventry City last time out. Mercer selected Mick Doyle at right half, Roy Cheetham droppin
to the bench. On fire right from the first whistle, City made the perfect start with a goal on thre
minutes when Colin Bell brilliantly flicked on a Neil Young throw-in for Summerbee to nonchalantl
head home.

Forest started the afternoon top of the table but rarely threatened as City's defence stood firm. Th
Blues, however, looked extremely dangerous with every attack. Forest 'keeper Peter Grummit was i
continuous action, but was powerless to prevent City extending their lead on twenty-three minute
when Coleman cracked a first-time drive into the roof of the net, leaving the young England prospec
helpless.

Deservedly two goals to the good at half-time, City were rampant on the resumption, completel
outplaying the visitors. With Summerbee creating numerous opportunities for Bell, Young an
Coleman, further goals seemed inevitable. To Forest's credit, they held firm and did come into th
game, but City's much maligned defence in recent weeks, superbly marshalled by George Heslop
denied any real opportunities. Demolishing a highly rated Forest side with an ease that bordered o
arrogance demonstrated the Blues' title potential, the scoreline not doing full justice to a superb Cit
performance. Summerbee created havoc amidst a normally solid Forest defence and Coleman an
Paul Hince provided cut and thrust from the wings, while Bell and Young were full of penetratio
and power.

This was definitely the sort of performance City fans, Mercer and Allison had been looking fo
Time would tell, but it was beginning to look possible that eleventh-placed City might be able t
challenge for Manchester United's First Division crown.

Manchester City 2   **Nottingham Forest 0**
  Summerbee
  Coleman

Manchester City: Dowd, Book, Pardoe, Doyle, Heslop, Oakes, Hince, Bell, Summerbee, Young, Coleman

Nottingham Forest: Grummitt, Hindley, Winfield, Hennessey, McKinley, Newton, Lyons, Chapman, Baker, Wignall, Moore

Manchester City v. Newcastle United

Football League First Division   **Date:** 6 September 1967   **Referee:** R. Kirkpatrick (Leicester)

Location: Maine Road, Manchester   **Attendance:** 29,978

City notched up a third consecutive victory in this hard-fought encounter, thanks to strikes by Paul Hince and Neil Young. With the impressive Mike Summerbee settling his long-running transfer and terms dispute, Joe Mercer had plenty to smile about after the Blues' 2-0 triumph that put them up to eighth place in the table.

City came into this game unchanged after a notable 2-0 win over Nottingham Forest, while mid-table Newcastle had drawn 1-1 against Stoke City. Although not at their most fluent, the Blues could have scored more than the two goals that came their way.

City fans expecting a spectacular performance as against Forest may have felt disappointed, but they did see flashes of inspiration that left them gasping with admiration. For long periods, City were masters of the costliest Newcastle side ever assembled – the Tynesiders having been put together for £500,000. Mercer, on the other hand, had spent just £134,000 on rebuilding the Blues.

Neil Yong notched Blues' second goal.

Hard work was at the bedrock of this victory, with Summerbee again leading a smooth-flowing forward line. The first goal, on thirty-three minutes, was scored by Hince, who slid home Alan Oakes' harmless-looking cross after Newcastle 'keeper Gordon Marshall dropped a clanger. The hapless Marshall was again at fault for City's second, on the hour, Young unleashing a thirty-yard drive that the Newcastle goalkeeper, for some reason, never attempted to save.

Young could have made the score more convincing had he not missed a penalty and Tony Coleman was guilty of blazing wide late on. Nevertheless, this was a terrific win for the Blues. City's defence was gaining in confidence with each game and had held one of the division's most potent attacks with ease. Heslop had dominated the much-feared Wyn Davies, while Tony Book, Glyn Pardoe and Oakes provided solid defensive cover as City ran out worthy winners.

Manchester City 2   **Newcastle United 0**

Hince

Young

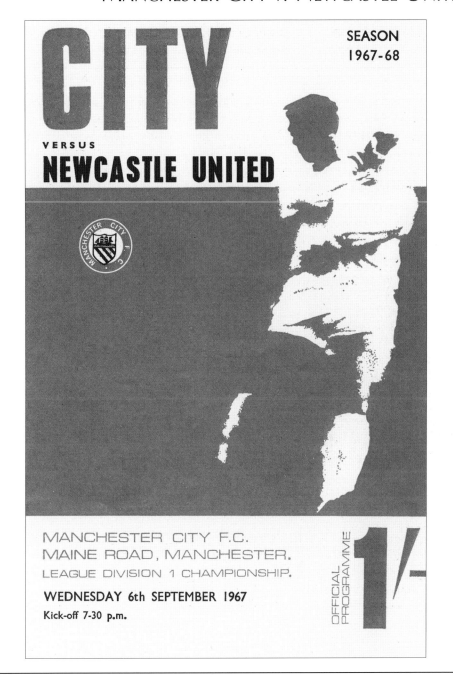

Manchester City: Dowd, Book, Pardoe, Doyle, Heslop, Oakes, Hince, Bell, Summerbee, Young, Coleman

Newcastle United: Marshall, Burton, Clarke, Elliot, McGrath, Iley, Scott, Bennett, Davies, Hilley, Robson

COVENTRY CITY v. MANCHESTER CITY

Football League First Division
Location: Highfield Road, Coventry

Date: 9 September 1967
Attendance: 34,578

Referee: H. New (Portsmouth)

Two quick-fire second-half goals by Mike Summerbee and Colin Bell sealed a fourth consecutive win for City against a lacklustre Sky Blues side and a first away victory this season. The Second Division Champions had not been finding top-flight football easy going and another scintillating display by Joe Mercer's charges put paid to any hopes Coventry had of building on their first victory of the season in midweek against Southampton. This win put the Blues, who beat Newcastle United 2-0 the previous Wednesday, up to fifth place, two points adrift of joint leaders Liverpool and Tottenham Hotspur. Making only one change to a line-up that had been extremely impressive in recent weeks, Mercer made David Connor substitute.

Dominating from the outset, City created numerous openings but had to wait until four minutes from half-time to open the scoring when Summerbee brilliantly controlled a through ball from Neil

Young before setting up Paul Hince, who slotted home neatly past overworked Coventry 'keeper Bill Glazier. Although the hosts showed more spirit and commitment on the resumption, nothing was going to stop rampant City. The Blues' second came from a Coleman free-kick on sixty-five minutes, Hince pushing the ball beyond Glazier for Summerbee to score with ease. Bell completed a comfortable victory in the seventy-first minute. Collecting a long pass from Mick Doyle, Bell waltzed past the entire Coventry defence before comprehensively beating Glazier for a superb solo effort.

This was another masterful performance by City, again displaying confidence and swagger. Superior in every department, their three-goal haul was fully deserved and clearly demonstrated why they were being touted as possible dark horses for the title.

Mick Doyle set up Colin Bell for a brilliant goal.

Coventry City 0

Manchester City 3
Summmberbee
Hince
Bell

Today's Teams

THE SKY BLUE

SKY BLUES

1 Bill GLAZIER
2 Mick KEARNS
3 Dietmar BRUCK
4 Brian LEWIS
5 Tony KNAPP
6 David CLEMENTS
7 John KEY
8 Ernie MACHIN
9 Bobby GOULD
10 John TUDOR
11 Ronnie REES
Sub:

MANCHESTER CITY
(Maroon Shirts & Shorts)

1 Harry DOWD
2 Tony BOOK
3 Glyn PARDOE
4 Michael DOYLE
5 George HESLOP
6 Alan OAKES
7 Paul HINCE
8 Colin BELL
9 Mike SUMMERBEE
10 Neil YOUNG
11 Tony COLEMAN
Sub: Roy CHEETHAM

Referee: H. G. New, Portsmouth.
Linesmen: F. Bellamy(Altrincham, Cheshire (red). J. H. Cope, London (orange).

1/- OFFICIAL MATCH DAY MAGAZINE
VOLUME 1
Number 4

COVENTRY CITY FOOTBALL CLUB

Coventry City: Glazier, Kearns, Bruck, Lewis, Knapp, Clements, Key, Carr, Gould, Tudor, Rees

Manchester City: Dowd, Book, Pardoe, Doyle, Heslop, Oakes, Hince, Bell, Summerbee, Young, Coleman

MANCHESTER CITY v. SHEFFIELD UNITED

Football League First Division   **Date:** 16 September 1967   **Referee:** T. Pallister (Peterlee)
Location: Maine Road, Manchester   **Attendance:** 31,922

Three brilliant goals in four sensational minutes made it five League wins on the trot for City. The Blues' 5-2 mauling of Sheffield United made it six successive wins for Joe Mercer's charges, who were now unbeaten at home in ten games. Third-placed City were now joint top alongside Liverpool, Arsenal, Sheffield Wednesday and Tottenham Hotspur. Having scored 17 goals in their last 5 home fixtures, the victory signalled beyond doubt the Blues' title credentials.

Rookie winger Stan Bowles notched a brace on his League debut, completing a remarkable few days that had seen him score twice on his full debut as a replacement for Tony Coleman during the Blues' midweek 4-0 League Cup demolition of Leicester City. Mercer's side, 3-0 winners at Coventry City in their last League match, were clear favourites to win against bottom-of-the-table Blades, who had lost 4-2 at Arsenal in their previous game.

Dominating from the start, City ended the game as a contest inside fifteen minutes with three quick-fire goals. The blitz started on twelve minutes with Bowles setting up Neil Young. Sixty seconds later, Mike Summerbee smashed in a second, before Colin Bell headed home a third after excellent work by Summerbee. Creating chance after chance, with Summerbee leading the line magnificently, Sheffield United did well to hang on and, credit to the Blades, their endeavour was rewarded on thirty-five minutes when Alan Woodward scored after Harry Dowd failed to punch clear when challenged by centre forward Mick Jones.

This was the first goal City had conceded in four games and, raising the tempo, they responded by scoring their fourth a minute from half-time with a flowing move. Instigated by Summerbee, Bell and Paul Hince combined before Mick Doyle's rasping thirty-five-yard shot hit the bar; Bowles headed in the rebound. City justifiably received a standing ovation from the near 32,000 crowd for a dazzling first-half display.

Within four minutes of the resumption, Sheffield reduced the deficit again, Gil Reece taking advantage of slack marking by the Blues defence. City quickly regained composure and remedied the slackness that had crept into their play with another goal after good work by Summerbee and Young, Bowles showing maturity beyond his years to steer a left-footed shot beyond Alan Hodgkinson for his second and City's fifth.

Dominating play again, with Alan Oakes bossing midfield and looking to go forward at every opportunity in search of more goals, City's superiority was such that even defenders George Heslop and Glynn Pardoe forced Hodgkinson into saves. Playing with panache and freedom, it looked like it would take a very good side to beat the Blues. Bell, Summerbee and Young may have been the catalyst in City's rise up the division, but on this particular afternoon debutant Bowles was by popular acclaim Man of the Match.

Manchester City 5	Sheffield United 2
Bowles (2), Summerbee	Woodward
Bell, Young	Reece

MANCHESTER CITY v. SHEFFIELD UNITED

Mike Summerbee evades a United defender.

Manchester City: Dowd, Book, Pardoe, Doyle, Heslop, Oakes, Hince, Bell, Summerbee, Young, Bowles

Sheffield United: Hodgkinson, Badger, Shaw, Munks, Matthewson, Mallender, Woodward, Fenoughty, Jones, Birchenall, Rees

ARSENAL v. MANCHESTER CITY

Football League First Division
Location: Highbury, London

Date: 23 September 1967
Attendance: 41,567

Referee: R. Pritchard (Salisbury)

Gunners striker John Radford settled this top-of-the-table clash with a first-half header, ending the Blues' five-match unbeaten First Division run. This was City's greatest test to date, facing an Arsenal side that possessed the second-best defensive League record, having conceded only 8 goals. The setback must have made Joe Mercer even more acutely aware that he needed to strengthen his team if they were to challenge the top sides.

Looking to build on their 5-2 mauling of Sheffield United, unchanged City knew they had a battle on their hands against high-flying Arsenal, who had enjoyed a 4-0 derby win over North London rivals Tottenham Hotspur the previous Saturday. Showing plenty of promise in the early stages, City were, however, unable to break through a well-organised Gunners defence.

The game's complexion changed when Arsenal opened the scoring through Radford from George Armstrong's left-wing corner on twenty-five minutes. City were under constant pressure and their response was to dish out rough treatment in their vain efforts to stem the tide, with Book the main culprit. His misdemeanours justifiably resulted in his name going into the referee's notebook in the thirty-fifth minute. With Mike Summerbee, so potent in recent weeks, well shackled by Terry Neill,

Glyn Pardoe.

Ian Ure and Frank McLintock, and the Blues' midfield unable to penetrate Arsenal's territory, Mercer must have been wondering how his team could ever pierce the Gunners' disciplined and organised defence.

To their credit, City came out after the interval with more purpose and nearly snatched an equaliser through Alan Oakes two minutes after the restart. The architect was Tony Coleman with a quick free-kick, but Oakes could only watch in disbelief as McLintock cleared his drive off the line, with Jim Furnell well beaten. Try as they might, the Blues could not break down an uncompromising Arsenal rearguard – despite a spirited fightback in the second half.

City were disappointed to have lost, but there was no real shame in this Highbury defeat as few sides could have overpowered Arsenal in this sort of form. Dropping down to fifth place in the table, Mercer would now be focusing on the Manchester derby coming up at Maine Road. The clash was to be City's first match of the campaign televised by BBC television's *Match of the Day* programme.

Arsenal 1
Radford

Manchester City 0

SEASON 1967-68

FOOTBALL LEAGUE DIVISION 1

F.A. CUP WINNERS
1930, 1936, 1950

LEAGUE CHAMPIONS
1931, 1933, 1934, 1935,
1938, 1948, 1953

THE FOOTBALL
LEAGUE TROPHY

ARSENAL

v

MANCHESTER CITY

SATURDAY 23rd September KICK-OFF 3 pm

ARSENAL STADIUM

Official Programme

6d

Arsenal: Furnell, Storey, Simpson, McLintock, Neill, Ure, Radford, Addison, Graham, Sammels, Armstrong

Manchester City: Dowd, Book, Pardoe, Doyle, Heslop, Oakes, Hince (Connor), Bell, Summerbee, Young, Coleman

MANCHESTER CITY v. MANCHESTER UNITED

Football League First Division   **Date:** 30 September 1967   **Referee:** K. Howley (Middlesbrough)
Location: Maine Road, Manchester   **Attendance:** 62,942

A Bobby Charlton brace broke City hearts after Colin Bell scored a fifth-minute opener for the Blues in a temperamental Manchester derby at Maine Road. The result saw City drop to sixth place in the table following a second defeat in a week.

This was the biggest game of the season to date for the City faithful and it brought a debut for goalkeeper Ken Mulhearn, recently joined from Stockport County. Also playing in their first derby fixture for City were Stan Bowles and Tony Coleman. The Blues were looking to bounce back from a one-goal defeat at Arsenal, while Manchester United were aiming to build on a hard-fought 1-0 win against Tottenham Hotspur on the previous Saturday.

City's start was electric. Blitzing the defending champions in a frenetic start, City deservedly opened the scoring through Bell within minutes. The goal came when a quick free-kick by Neil Young was collected by Mick Doyle, who ran at the retreating United defence. Sprinting into the penalty area, Bell cracked Doyle's stroked pass into the right corner of the net past a diving Alex Stepney.

City continued to dominate and several times had Stepney at full stretch. However, United got their passing game together and their persistence paid off with a goal in the twenty-first minute when Charlton raced through a static City defence to slide home a centre from George Best.

Thirteen minutes later United took the lead, when a mistake by Doyle enabled Charlton to collect the ball and slide it beyond the despairing reach of Mulhearn. City were stunned to be hit by two sucker-punches after enjoying so much possession. Joe Mercer's team continued to press forward and could count themselves unfortunate to be trailing 2-1 at half-time, having been the superior side.

Second-half action was end to end, with United looking the more comfortable but the game erupted in the sixty-third minute, Young limping off after a hefty challenge to be replaced by Stan Horne. With tempers flaring all over the park, referee Mr Howley needed eyes in the back of his head to keep the game under control. Bowles and Brian Kidd had to be separated by local police after coming to blows. Both players were booked. On the field, United never looked like relinquishing their grip on a game that had started brightly before degenerating into a scrappy affair.

City's second loss on the bounce was a real concern for boss Mercer and coach Malcolm Allison as the Blues' recent winning run was starting to seem a distant memory. Supporters were hoping transfer rumours concerning Bolton striker Francis Lee would prove more than just tittle-tattle.

Manchester City 1   **Manchester United 2**
Bell   Charlton (2)

MANCHESTER CITY v. MANCHESTER UNITED

Tony Coleman challenges Pat Crerand for the ball.

Manchester City: Mulhearn, Book, Pardoe, Doyle, Heslop, Oakes, Bowles, Bell, Summerbee, Young (Horne), Coleman

Manchester United: Stepney, Dunne, Burns, Crerand, Foulkes (Aston), Stiles, Best, Sadler, Charlton, Law, Kidd

CITY

SEASON
1967-68

VERSUS

MANCHESTER UNITED

MANCHESTER CITY F.C.
MAINE ROAD, MANCHESTER.
LEAGUE DIVISION 1 CHAMPIONSHIP.
SATURDAY, 30th SEPTEMBER 1967
Kick-off 3-0 p.m.

OFFICIAL PROGRAMME

1/-

SUNDERLAND *v.* MANCHESTER CITY

Football League First Division   **Date:** 7 October 1967   **Referee:** K. Styles (Barnsley)
Location: Roker Park, Sunderland   **Attendance:** 27,885

A freak Neil Martin goal on thirty minutes handed Sunderland a first win in five outings as the Blues' helter-skelter season continued with a third consecutive defeat. Amid rumours sweeping Maine Road that Bolton striker Francis Lee would sign and make his debut against the Wearsiders, City fans headed to the North East hoping his renowned finishing power would get the Blues back on track in the title race. However, on a day when City missed a hatful of chances, there was no sign of Lee and no points as the Blues dropped to ninth in the table.

The Blues started with just one change from last week's loss against Manchester United, Stan Horne replacing Mick Doyle. City's centre-back dropped to the bench, presumably paying the price for his error that cost a goal against the Reds. Sunderland, who lost 3-0 at Tottenham Hotspur on the previous Saturday, were unchanged.

City made a whirlwind start, but Horne, Mike Summerbee, Stan Bowles and Alan Oakes all spurned early chances. Leading a charmed life, Jim Montgomery was in early action as a Colin Bell header struck the bar before Summerbee was left rueing his luck, Cecil Irwin clearing his goalbound shot off the line with the Sunderland 'keeper beaten. Sporadic attacks from the Wearsiders came to nothing before Tony Coleman hit the woodwork again for City.

Against the run of play, Sunderland took the lead on the half-hour. Colin Suggett and Jim Baxter made the opportunity for Martin and the centre forward's finish summed up the Blues' current luck, the ball striking a post and bouncing across the goal before rolling into the opposite corner to the amazement of goalkeeper Ken Mulhearn. Gaining confidence, Sunderland forced Mulhearn into a couple of smart saves before half-time but on the resumption one team dominated. A City equaliser seemed inevitable, but with Montgomery growing in confidence and Charlie Hurley, playing his first senior game for seven months, in glorious form, Sunderland held firm. Hurley capped an outstanding performance with a brilliant interception to thwart Neil Young in the closing moments.

Although Joe Mercer's team dominated midfield through Oakes and Horne, the Blues' attackers, so prolific a few weeks prior, had lacked the guile and punch to put away opportunities.

On a day when two points went begging for the Blues, Mercer's signing of Lee could not come quickly enough for City followers.

Sunderland 1   **Manchester City 0**
Martin

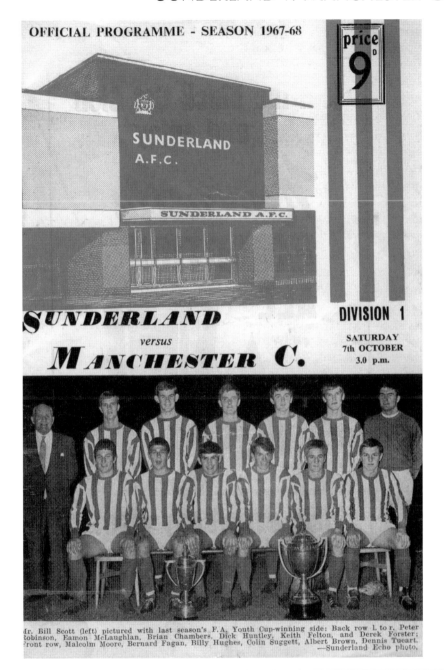

OFFICIAL PROGRAMME - SEASON 1967-68

price 9D

SUNDERLAND
A.F.C.

SUNDERLAND A.F.C.

SUNDERLAND

DIVISION 1

versus

MANCHESTER C.

SATURDAY
7th OCTOBER
3.0 p.m.

Mr. Bill Scott (left) pictured with last season's F.A. Youth Cup-winning side; Back row l. to r. Peter Robinson, Eamon McLaughlan, Brian Chambers, Dick Huntley, Keith Felton, and Derek Forster; front row, Malcolm Moore, Bernard Fagan, Billy Hughes, Colin Suggett, Albert Brown, Dennis Tueart.
—Sunderland Echo photo.

Sunderland: Montgomery, Irwin, Parke, Todd, Hurley, Baxter, Suggett, Kinnell, Martin, B. Heslop, Brand

Manchester City: Mulhearn, Book, Pardoe, Horne, Heslop, Oakes, Bowles, Bell, Summerbee, Young, Coleman

MANCHESTER CITY v. WOLVERHAMPTON WANDERERS

Football League First Division   **Date:** 14 October 1967   **Referee:** P. Partridge (Middlesbrough)
Location: Maine Road, Manchester   **Attendance:** 36,476

Goals by Mick Doyle and Neil Young got City back to winning ways as Francis Lee finally made his debut, following a much-publicised £60,000 move from Bolton Wanderers. The Blues' 2-0 win lifted them to eighth place in the table, four points behind leaders Liverpool.

With negotiations completed, Joe Mercer included Lee in his starting line-up against Wolves, replacing Paul Hince. Two further changes from the midweek League Cup draw with Blackpool saw Mick Doyle come in for Stan Horne at right half, while Ken Mulhearn was back in goal following rookie 'keeper Joe Corrigan's first-team debut against the Seasiders.

Heavy rain did nothing to dampen the spirits of a near 37,000 crowd, who were convinced City would bounce back from their surprise loss at Sunderland the previous week.

Wolves, who had drawn 2-2 with Newcastle United, started the game with spirit and flair, putting City under early pressure before new boy Lee linked smartly with Mike Summerbee, Lee going close with his first meaningful shot in a City shirt after eight minutes. On the ten-minute mark Doyle opened the scoring following good work by Tony Coleman, Doyle forcing his way between two Wolves defenders before thumping a terrific shot past Wolves 'keeper Phil Parkes.

Undaunted, the visitors put City under pressure, with former Blues favourite Wagstaffe looking sharp, but both sides failed to convert chances before Young extended City's lead on twenty-two minutes when Parkes failed to hold a Bell cross-shot. Young was on hand to hook the loose ball home.

The second half again saw both sides miss chances, with Wolves in particular unfortunate not to reduce the deficit. Derek Dougan had a header ruled out for offside thirteen minutes from time before Alan Evans latched on to a poor clearance by Mulhearn only to see his goal-bound shot kicked off the line by the attentive Glynn Pardoe.

With Wolves attacking at will, City looked to put the result beyond doubt but again spurned gilt-edged chances. Bell blazed wide; Young screwed a good opportunity beyond the far post while Summerbee missed a sitter after being set up by Lee with the 'keeper beaten.

This was a welcome win for City but criticism of their woeful finishing was widespread. Nevertheless, with Lee making an impressive bow, the Blues were looking a more balanced side and Mercer was satisfied with the result.

Manchester City 2   Wolverhampton Wanderers 0
  Doyle
  Young

MANCHESTER CITY v. WOLVERHAMPTON WANDERERS

CITY

VERSUS

WOLVERHAMPTON W.

SEASON
1967-68

MANCHESTER CITY F.C.
MAINE ROAD, MANCHESTER.
LEAGUE DIVISION 1 CHAMPIONSHIP.

SATURDAY, 14th OCTOBER 1967
Kick-off 3-0 p.m.

OFFICIAL PROGRAMME **1/-**

Manchester City: Mulhearn, Book, Pardoe, Doyle, Heslop, Oakes, Lee, Bell, Summerbee, Young, Coleman (Clay)

Wolverhampton Wanderers: Parkes, Taylor, Thomson, Bailey, Woodfield, Holsgrove, Wharton, Knowles, Dougan, Evans, Wagstaffe (Burnside)

Fulham v. Manchester City

Football League First Division   **Date:** 21 October 1967   **Referee:** P. Pye (Bedford)
Location: Craven Cottage, London   **Attendance:** 22,108

Four second-half goals secured the points for City in an action-packed encounter at Craven Cottage. Leading the way for the Blues was Mike Summerbee with a brace. Neil Young also found the target but the biggest cheer was reserved for Francis Lee, striking his first City goal. Steve Earle and Jimmy Conway scored Fulham's consolation goals. The Blues' 4-2 win took them up to sixth place in the table, just three points behind leaders Liverpool.

With Glyn Pardoe sidelined, David Connor stepped into an otherwise unchanged line-up from the team that had defeated Wolves a week earlier. Fulham, who had lost 2-1 at Newcastle United the previous Saturday, named an unchanged team.

Although dominant in the first half, Joe Mercer's side was guilty of missing a number of chances. The Blues' superior skill and ability posed serious problems for Fulham, who started the afternoon joint bottom of the table, but at the half-time break, Mercer must have been seriously dissatisfied with his players' inability to turn possession into goals – Summerbee, Young and Colin Bell were all guilty.

Within minutes of the restart, City at last made their class tell with two quick-fire goals in the space of four minutes. Summerbee opened the scoring on forty-nine minutes when he neatly headed home a Bell cross before Young punished Fulham after 'keeper Ian Seymour failed to hold on to a Tony Coleman cross. To their credit, however, Fulham reduced the arrears on fifty-seven minutes when Earle found a gap in a crowded City goalmouth with Ken Mulhearn unsighted. Fired up, the Londoners battled away but both teams' over-exuberance forced Referee Pye to stop the game and warn several players to calm down.

On sixty-three minutes City restored their two-goal advantage when Lee and Coleman combined; the Blues winger providing an inch-perfect cross for Summerbee to head home his second goal of the afternoon. Undeterred, Fulham set up a tense finish six minutes from time when Conway reduced the deficit again, firing Les Barratt's cross past Mulhearn. The Blues were not to be denied though and Lee was rewarded for his efforts in the closing moments when he created a goal from nothing, shooting past a startled Seymour.

This was a deserved City victory, but sloppy finishing threatened a game that should have been won by the interval. Nevertheless, the Blues were moving forward following a second consecutive win.

Fulham 2	Manchester City 4
Earle	Summerbee (2)
Conway	Young
	Lee

Fulham: Seymour, Mealand, Dempsey, Ryan, Callaghan, Conway, Brown, Earle, Clarke, Haynes, Barratt

Manchester City: Mulhearn, Book, Connor, Doyle, Heslop, Oakes, Lee, Bell, Summerbee, Young, Coleman

Manchester City v. Leeds United

Football League First Division **Date:** 28 October 1967 **Referee:** E. Jennings (Stourbridge)
Location: Maine Road, Manchester **Attendance:** 39,713

The Blues snatched a terrific win against one of the First Division title favourites with a Colin Bell header four minutes from time. Bell may have been the goalscoring hero of the afternoon, but City's win would have been greater if it was not for a brilliant performance from Leeds United's Welsh international goalkeeper Gary Sprake. City's third successive victory moved them up to fourth place, behind Manchester United and Sheffield Wednesday and three points adrift of front-runners Liverpool.

City, 4-2 winners at Fulham the Saturday before, and Leeds, who had defeated Newcastle United 2-0 that day, came into the match in confident mood. The Yorkshire team set the early pace and Ken Mulhearn was forced into action to stop a fierce drive from Albert Johanneson. For long periods, Don Revie's talented team dictated play as City's attack struggled to make inroads, while striker Mick Jones, making his fifth start for Leeds since a £100,000 transfer from Sheffield United, gave the Blues' defence a torrid time leading the line.

After thirty minutes City finally began to shake off their early lethargy, but could not get the ball past Leeds' solid defence. Only Liverpool had conceded fewer goals to date, and this was due in no small part to the presence of the athletic Sprake in goal. Here, he saved fierce drives from Neil Young and Mike Summerbee to frustrate the majority of a partisan Maine Road crowd, before making a brilliant stop to deny Young again and tipping a rising shot from Tony Coleman over the bar.

Encouraged, City started the second period in fine style but were left to rue their luck in the opening minutes when Sprake turned a Summerbee shot behind before denying Bell, who had had the ball headed into his path by Mick Doyle from the resultant corner, with a sensational point-blank save.

In control, a goal looked inevitable for Joe Mercer's team, but the Leeds rearguard stood firm. Brilliantly saving a Francis Lee drive, Sprake blocked another City effort, but as he lay stranded on the ground a goal seemed certain when the ball fell at the feet of Bell. However, with an open goal to aim at, his shot was somehow deflected behind by left-back Terry Cooper.

Leeds' battling display appeared to have earned them the point they had come to take back across the Pennines, but City finally got the goal their non-stop effort deserved on eighty-six minutes when the majestic Bell headed Summerbee's pinpoint cross from the right flank past a despairing Sprake to claim the win.

Only Sprake had stood between them and a hatful of goals and, as the game wore on, George Heslop in City's defence had made Jones look anything but an England striker. Defeating one of the up-and-coming teams must surely have given the Blues tremendous confidence.

Manchester City 1 **Leeds United 0**
Bell

Manchester City: Mulhearn, Book, Pardoe, Doyle, Heslop, Oakes, Lee, Bell, Summerbee, Young, Coleman

Leeds United: Sprake, Reaney, Cooper, Madeley, Charlton, Hunter, Greenhoff, Lorimer, Jones, Gray, Johanneson

EVERTON v. MANCHESTER CITY

Football League First Division   **Date:** 4 November 1967   **Referee:** E. Wallace (Swindon)
Location: Goodison Park, LIverpool   **Attendance:** 47,144

Classy City earned a share of the spoils in a 1-1 draw at Goodison Park, courtesy of a David Connor strike, but left the Merseysiders regretting their misfortune following a disputed second-half equaliser by Everton inside-right Ernie Hunt.

In a hard-fought encounter, Everton's England World Cup star Alan Ball also missed a penalty but the main talking point was Hunt's goal, which looked suspiciously offside. Nevertheless, Joe Mercer was satisfied as his team, unbeaten in four games, remained in fourth place, three points behind League leaders Liverpool.

Surprising many pundits, Mercer made a late tactical switch following City's impressive 1-0 win over Leeds United the previous Saturday, omitting inside forward Neil Young in preference to utility player Connor, who was given the key task of shadowing Ball as he did last season.

Everton, who had lost 1-0 at Newcastle United the week before, enjoyed the lion's share of possession early on with debutant forward Aiden Maher seeing plenty of action. Ball in particular was causing problems with a number of dangerous crosses into the heart of City's defence, but George Heslop and Alan Oakes stood firm to prevent Everton from capitalising on constant pressure.

Against the run of play, City opened the scoring on thirty-one minutes when Connor shot City into the lead after a swift counterattack. Coleman started the move with a high cross and Mike Summerbee combined with Francis Lee before Connor shot firmly past Gordon West. Stung into action, Everton upped the tempo and tempers quickly became frayed amid wild challenges from a number of players, necessitating the referee to warn both teams to calm down. Everton should have equalised on the stroke of half-time when Mick Doyle was adjudged to have brought down Hunt, but Ball pulled the resultant spot-kick wide, to the dismay of the home supporters.

On the resumption, City more than held their own and should have extended their one-goal advantage on fifty-eight minutes when Bell wasted a golden chance. Having instigated the opportunity when he collected a clearance by Everton full-back Sandy Brown, Bell found himself with an open goal in front of him after Lee had squared the ball past West. Somehow, though, Brown got back to block Bell's effort. Everton made the Blues pay dearly within three minutes when Hunt scored his controversial equaliser. With Doyle off the field receiving treatment, Everton took advantage of Doyle's absence when Ball sent Hunt clear to calmly slot the ball past Ken Mulhearn. City players protested bitterly to the referee but to no avail. Encouraged, Everton pushed hard for a winner but City's defence held firm, Heslop thwarting Joe Royle, while Mulhearn saved well from Maher.

On balance, a draw was just about the right result in spite of questions regarding the validity of Everton's goal. The Blues' defence had again showed their undoubted qualities, whilst Bell, Summerbee and Lee linked superbly in attack.

Everton 1   **Manchester City 1**

Hunt   Connor

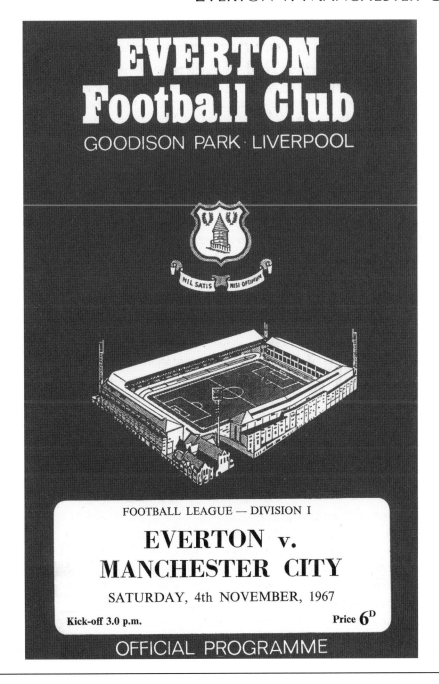

EVERTON Football Club

GOODISON PARK · LIVERPOOL

NIL SATIS NISI OPTIMUM

FOOTBALL LEAGUE — DIVISION I

EVERTON v. MANCHESTER CITY

SATURDAY, 4th NOVEMBER, 1967

Kick-off 3.0 p.m.   Price **6**^{D}

OFFICIAL PROGRAMME

Everton: West, Brown, Wilson, Kendall, Labone, Harvey, Ball, Hunt (Royle), Young, Hurst, Maher

Manchester City: Mulhearn, Book, Pardoe, Doyle, Heslop, Oakes, Lee, Bell, Summerbee, Connor, Coleman

MANCHESTER CITY v. LEICESTER CITY

Football League First Division   **Date:** 11 Novermber 1967   **Referee:** D. Payne (Sheffield)
Location: Maine Road, Manchester   **Attendance:** 29,039

Six-hitting City signalled their title aspirations with a breathtaking performance at Maine Road. Luckless Leicester City were unfortunate to run into Joe Mercer's team on an afternoon when they produced the best attacking spectacle by any team this season. City's display was packed with power, lethal finishing and superb individual ability. Two goals apiece from Neil Young and Francis Lee, together with strikes by Mick Doyle and Alan Oakes, swept Leicester away as the Blues climbed into third spot, just two points behind new League leaders Manchester United. Liverpool lay in second place.

Both teams had picked up a point the previous Saturday: City at Everton, Leicester in a 2-2 thriller at home to Newcastle United. With Heslop missing his first start of the League campaign, Stan Horne came in at centre half for City and, somewhat surprisingly, flu-ridden Young made the starting line-up – despite having spent most of the week in isolation. Leicester remained unchanged.

City ripped into Leicester from the kick-off and deservedly scored twice in six minutes. Oakes hammered home the first on three minutes, following a Coleman free-kick from just outside the Leicester penalty area, before Young notched his first goal with a fine left-foot shot from close range after a slick exchange of passes between Book, Lee and Summerbee.

Despite City being in control, Leicester created chances. Nish hit the bar with a lob and new signing Frank Large saw a good header dealt with impressively by the ever-alert Mulhearn. Mercer's team, however, sensed goals. Creating numerous chances with nifty approach work from Lee, Bell Summerbee and Coleman, City went further ahead on thirty-four minutes when Bell back-headed a Lee centre into the path of Young, who scored with ease. Three minutes later the game was over as a contest, City grabbing a fourth when Doyle rifled Summerbee's pass past a despairing Peter Shilton Exultant City supporters gave their heroes a standing ovation at half-time.

City resumed where they had left off in the second half, with both Oakes and Pardoe joining in the attacking frenzy, such was City's dominance. Leicester's beleaguered 'keeper Shilton brilliantly saved a rising drive by Lee but there was no letup in the Blues' ceaseless attack and Lee added his name to the list of scorers with City's fifth, swooping onto a poor back-pass from Bobby Roberts before thundering the ball into the top corner of the net.

Despite spirited Leicester resistance, City battered away, determined to top the five goals they scored against Sheffield United in September, and got their just reward four minutes from time Coleman carved an opening with a brilliant ball to Lee, City's sharpshooter wrong-footing Shilton to complete the rout.

Summerbee, Bell and Young played with authority, while Lee was proving his worth with each game. Every City player had impressed in a sensational exhibition of attacking football but it was Oakes who shaded the Man of the Match honours.

Manchester City 6   **Leicester City 0**
  Young (2), Lee (2)
  Oakes, Doyle

Manchester City: Mulhearn, Book, Pardoe, Doyle, Horne, Oakes, Lee, C. Bell, Summerbee, Young, Coleman

Leicester City: Shilton, Rodrigues, Norman, Roberts, Woollett, W. Bell, Sinclair, Nish, Large, Gibson, Stringfellow

West Ham United v. Manchester City

Football League First Division　　**Date:** 18 November 1967　　**Referee:** W. Gow (Swansea)
Location: Upton Park, London　　**Attendance:** 25,595

Francis Lee's second brace in a week claimed a superb victory as the Blues made it five wins in six games. Lee's two-goal salvo must have impressed watching England boss Alf Ramsey as rampant City racked up a third away win of the campaign to leave them in third place, two points behind League leaders Manchester United. Sir Alf was at Upton Park, checking on the form of Hammers trio Moore, Hurst and Peters and the City duo of Mike Summerbee and Colin Bell, but Lee starred in the Blues' 3-2 win.

George Heslop returned to the side after the previous week's 6-0 mauling of Leicester City, replacing Stan Horne, who dropped to the bench. West Ham, who had lost 1-0 at Newcastle United, included new signings Bobby Ferguson and John Cushley. The Hammers could also boast the division's top scorer in World Cup hero Geoff Hurst, who had 11 goals going into the game.

Both teams started confidently. However, City slowly gained control and grabbed the initiative with two quick-fire goals, the first on twenty-four minutes. Moving at pace, Tony Coleman combined with Bell and Summerbee before skipper Tony Book chipped a neat cross to Lee, who superbly hooked the ball past a motionless Ferguson. With City attacking at will, a rasping drive from Bell was well saved by Ferguson but, from the resultant corner by Coleman, Summerbee outjumped John Cushley to head the ball beyond the Hammers 'keeper.

Undeterred, West Ham hit back inside two minutes, Peters ghosting in to nod home a pinpoint free-kick by John Sissons after Book fouled the winger. Looking lively, Hammers' Peter Brabrook forced Ken Mulhearn into a good save before George Heslop appeared to impede Hurst in the six-yard box; referee Gow turned down home appeals for a penalty. The last action of an enthralling half saw Neil Young shoot on the turn just over the West Ham bar.

From the restart, City had a good shout for a penalty turned down by Gow when Frank Lampard pulled down Coleman. With both teams attacking at will, a goal seemed inevitable and City took advantage on the hour when they re-established their two-goal cushion. Heslop instigated the opening by dispossessing Brabrook inside West Ham's half. A neat pass found Lee, who needed no invitation to take the ball forward before placing it wide of the advancing Ferguson.

With chances at both ends, Ferguson denied Young to keep his team in the game, before a Peters effort bounced off a City post. The Blues were still trying to increase their lead and Lee looked to have completed his hat-trick only to see his shot hooked off the line by Lampard.

Slackness in the City defence allowed Hurst to pull a goal back for West Ham on seventy-six minutes and, shortly after, Mulhearn left a lob from Moore to go over the top only to see the ball suddenly dip and bounce back off the bar into play.

West Ham United 2	Manchester City 3
Peters	Lee (2)
Hurst	Summerbee

West Ham United v. Manchester City

Franny Lee scored two great goals.

Made to fight all the way, this was a tremendous City triumph, having survived a late rally from the Hammers. Once again, the Blues showed character and gave an exhilarating display of attacking football that saw them dubbed the most attractive side in England.

West Ham United: Ferguson, Lampard, Burkett, Peters, Cushley, Moore, Redknapp, Boyce, Brabrook, Hurst, Sissons

Manchester City: Mulhearn, Book, Pardoe, Doyle, Heslop, Oakes, Lee, Bell, Summerbee, Young, Coleman

WEST HAM
UNITED

BOLEYN GROUND : LONDON E.13

No. 19

MANCHESTER CITY

FOOTBALL LEAGUE : Division I

SATURDAY 18th NOVEMBER 1967 at 3 p.m.

OFFICIAL PROGRAMME 6ᴰ

MANCHESTER CITY v. BURNLEY

ootball League First Division   **Date:** 25 November 1967   **Referee:** J. Finney (Wellington)
ocation: Maine Road, Manchester   **Attendance:** 36,925

wo goals by winger Tony Coleman secured the Blues' sixth victory in seven games as their title hallenge gathered pace. Consolidating third position, just one point adrift of Manchester United, ne First Division's top entertainers had now scored 13 goals in the last 3 games, Mike Summerbee, ony Coleman (2) and Neil Young completing a 4-2 victory for Joe Mercer's title pretenders.

Fielding the side that claimed a 3-2 win at West Ham the Saturday before, City made a whirlwind tart, opening the scoring inside twenty seconds. Burnley, 2-0 winners against Newcastle United the revious week, kicked off but Alan Oakes intercepted before putting Glynn Pardoe in possession. oung headed on the left-back's pass to Colin Bell. Summerbee gave Harry Thomson no chance vith a firm header from Bell's pinpoint cross.

Looking for better luck on their travels, having been thumped 8-1 at West Brom two weeks before, ne visitors were unfortunate within seconds of the restart when referee Finney ruled out an equaliser or offside. Burnley were made to pay with a second goal on six minutes when Colin Waldron cythed Lee down from behind after a brilliant dribble into the penalty area. Coleman scored from ne resultant penalty.

Playing with pace and panache, City forwards were slicing through the Burnley defence at will. One magical piece of Young brilliance had the crowd on its feet: collecting the ball from Pardoe, e sent two Burnley defenders sprawling with a graceful swerve before placing his shot just wide of he far post. Under a barrage of attacks, Burnley tempers frayed and after a number of fouls Waldron nad his name taken for slashing down Summerbee.

The early pace had enabled Burnley to get into the game, but they did not possess the skill to rouble City, who stretched their lead on the stroke of half-time; Young unleashing a vicious left-foot hot into the corner of the net after Lee and Summerbee outwitted the visitors' porous defence. For he second consecutive home game, the Blues departed at half-time to a standing ovation and City ans were soon cheering another goal on fifty-one minutes.

The Blues' fourth goal came after David Merrington was harshly adjudged to have handled the all following a tussle with Bell. Thomson stopped Lee's penalty kick, but Coleman hit the ball home off the bar. With only pride to play for Colin Blant replaced Gary France.

Brian O'Neill forced a neat save from Mulhearn before Caspar beat the 'keeper with a low shot on he hour to maintain his record of scoring in every game this season. Continuing to press, Burnley's persistence paid off a minute from time when Morgan slotted the ball into the Blues' net after Blant pounced on a poor back-pass by Coleman to Mulhearn.

Despite Burnley's two strikes, this was another brilliant performance by City, who blitzed Burnley n the first half. Oakes and Summerbee dictated play, ably assisted by Lee, Bell, Coleman and the

Manchester City 4	Burnley 2
Summerbee	Casper
Coleman (2)	Morgan
Young	

Manchester City v. Burnley

Tony Coleman notched two goals.

graceful Young. However, Mercer would have to ponder how his team allowed battered opponents back into the game after dominating.

Manchester City: Mulhearn, Book, Pardoe, Doyle, Heslop, Oakes, Lee, Bell, Summerbee, Young, Coleman

Burnley: Thomson, Angus, Latcham, O'Neill, Waldron, Merrington, Morgan, France (Blant), Lockhead, Bellamy, Casper

CITY

VERSUS

BURNLEY

SEASON
1967-68

MANCHESTER CITY F.C.
MAINE ROAD, MANCHESTER.

LEAGUE DIVISION 1 CHAMPIONSHIP.

SATURDAY, 25th NOVEMBER, 1967

Kick-off 3-0 p.m.

OFFICIAL PROGRAMME 1/-

SHEFFIELD WEDNESDAY v. MANCHESTER CITY

Football League First Division
Location: Hillsborough, Sheffield

Date: 2 December 1967
Attendance: 38,137

Referee: J. Taylor (Wolverhampton)

Controversy raged at Hillsborough following a last-gasp goal that denied City a fourth consecutive win. Joe Mercer's team looked set to continue their winning streak, but saw victory cruelly snatched away when Wednesday's Johnny Fantham equalised deep into injury time. City supporters were convinced Fantham had handled before beating Ken Mulhearn. Nevertheless, the Blues remained in third spot, two points behind Manchester United.

Mercer named the same eleven that had defeated Burnley 4-2 the previous Saturday. Owl boss Alan Brown looked for his sixth-placed side to show an improvement from a 4-0 drubbing at Newcastle United.

Starting brightly, City created early opportunities with Mike Summerbee causing havoc amongst the Wednesday defence. City's flyer was in fine form and unfortunate not to open the scoring when Wilf Smith blocked his goal-bound shot on the line with Peter Springett beaten. Neil Young also went close after Springett collided with two defenders before the ball was finally cleared.

The Blues' impressive start was marred when Jack Whitham tackled Summerbee heavily on eight minutes. Following lengthy treatment, Summerbee returned as City continued to press. Wednesday blocked efforts by Mick Doyle and Alan Oakes before coming into the game as an attacking force with a Whitham strike and a Smith header causing panic in the City rearguard.

Ending the half strongly, Wednesday looked the more likely to score with Fantham, Whitham and Smith all going close. Spectators, however, hardly had a chance to return to their seats after the break before City took the lead, Oakes thumping a great strike into the roof of the net past a motionless Springett from a deft pass by Young. Picking up the pace, Colin Bell had an opportunity to double City's advantage but shot straight at Springett. Francis Lee volleyed the rebound into what appeared to be an empty net only to see Sam Ellis brilliantly head clear. Refusing to yield, Wednesday pressure forced Mulhearn into a brilliant point-blank save from John Ritchie before his defence came to the rescue, blocking Jim McCalliog's shot on the line.

Although under constant pressure late on, the Blues looked capable of holding on until deep into injury time when Fantham ran onto a Young pass to outstrip the City defence and beat Mulhearn. Despite Blues' protestations, the goal was allowed to stand. Wednesday's late equaliser ended an explosive match. A point may have been lost but it could not detract from another superb performance, with Doyle enjoying arguably his best game of the season.

Sheffield Wednesday 1
Fantham

Manchester City 1
Oakes

FOOTBALL LEAGUE—DIVISION I

MANCHESTER CITY

On Saturday, 2nd December, 1967, kick-off 3.0 p.m.

at Hillsborough

Sheffield Wednesday: Springett, Smith, Megson, Mobley, Ellis, Young, Whitham, Fantham, Ritchie, McCalliog, Eustace

Manchester City: Mulhearn, Book, Pardoe, Doyle, Heslop, Oakes, Lee, Bell, Summerbee, Young, Coleman

MANCHESTER CITY v. TOTTENHAM HOTSPUR

Football League First Division   **Date:** 9 December 1967   **Referee:** D. Smith (Stonehouse)
Location: Maine Road, Manchester   **Attendance:** 35,792

Any doubts that the Blues were genuine title challengers disappeared after this dazzling four-goal performance. On a snow-covered, rock-hard pitch that many thought unplayable, City produced a performance described by manager Joe Mercer as the best since his arrival at Maine Road. A goal behind to a Jimmy Greaves special, City rattled in four to bury a Tottenham Hotspur side that itself had pretensions to the title. City's goals tally of 45 in 20 games had now eclipsed by two last season's total. The Blues were still third, but now just one point behind joint leaders Manchester United and Liverpool.

Both teams came into the match on the back of 1-1 draws the week before, City at Sheffield Wednesday, fifth-placed Tottenham against Newcastle United. With conditions underfoot treacherous, an unchanged City came out twenty minutes before kick-off to get the feel of the perilous surface.

A weather-affected crowd of just over 35,000 saw both sets of players struggle from the outset to get a grip with their studs, sliding and stumbling on the frozen pitch.

Nevertheless, Tottenham took the lead on six minutes when Greaves slotted home Terry Venables' deflected free-kick after George Heslop had fouled Frank Saul just outside the penalty area. Undeterred, and finding their feet, City tore into the Londoners. Neil Young, Mike Summerbee and Tony Coleman had efforts smothered by the Tottenham defence before City deservedly equalised on seventeen minutes after both Francis Lee and Summerbee had had shots blocked in an almighty goalmouth scramble, Colin Bell cracking home Alan Mullery's half-hit clearance.

Although in control, and running at will through the Tottenham rearguard, the score remained 1-1 at half-time. However, blitzing their opponents on the restart, Lee, Bell and Summerbee all went close before City deservedly took the lead on fifty minutes. Mick Doyle dispossessed Cliff Jones in midfield and Young floated in a perfect centre for Summerbee to send a looping header past Pat Jennings. Two minutes later the crossbar shuddered to Young's powerful drive. Not to be denied, and seemingly oblivious to deteriorating conditions, a third City goal arrived just past the hour when Coleman knocked the ball into an empty net after Jennings deflected a Lee strike onto the foot of a post. On seventy-five minutes, rampaging City secured the points, Young tapping home after Jennings had saved a Bell drive.

The Blues had outclassed a Tottenham side packed with internationals and the final score only served to prove City's dominance on a pitch that few could walk on, let alone play football. But for the bravery of Jennings' and Dave Mackay, the final score could have been a massacre.

Summerbee, Lee and Bell excelled in atrocious conditions while Tony Book, Heslop and the rapidly maturing Doyle impressed in a City performance dubbed the 'Ballet on Ice' after being watched by around five million viewers on *Match of the Day*. It was to be the programme's 'Match of the Season', City receiving national acclaim. Almost three decades on, it is still viewed as a classic.

Manchester City 4   **Tottenham Hotspur 1**
Bell, Summerbee   Greaves
Coleman, Young

SEASON 1967-68

CITY

VERSUS

TOTTENHAM HOTSPUR

MANCHESTER CITY F.C.
MAINE ROAD, MANCHESTER.
LEAGUE DIVISION 1 CHAMPIONSHIP.

SATURDAY, 9th DECEMBER, 1967
Kick-off 3-0 p.m.

OFFICIAL PROGRAMME 1/-

Manchester City: Mulhearn, Book, Pardoe, Doyle, Heslop, Oakes, Lee, Bell, Summerbee, Young, Coleman

Tottenham Hotspur: Jennings, Kinnear, Knowles, Mullery, Hoy, Mackay, Saul, Greaves, Gilzean, Venables, Jones

LIVERPOOL v. MANCHESTER CITY

Football League First Division
Location: Anfield, Liverpool

Date: 16 December 1967
Attendance: 53,268

Referee: V. James (York)

Francis Lee gained City a share of the spoils with a predator's strike sixteen minutes from tim in a pulsating top-of-the-table encounter at Anfield. Halfway through the League campaign, bot sides demonstrated why they would be in the shakeup for English football's top prize. Howeve Manchester United's 3-1 win over Everton extended their lead at the top to two points.

After playing Sparta Prague in a friendly at Maine Road during midweek, Joe Mercer named a ful strength side, while Liverpool made one change, Geoff Strong coming in for stalwart centre-bac Ron Yeats. With Liverpool's Tommy Lawrence and Roger Hunt delayed due to pre-match traffic, capacity crowd, including England boss Alf Ramsey, waited patiently for this eagerly anticipate fixture. The clash was viewed as a decisive test for the Blues' championship credentials, as they la behind second-placed Liverpool only on goal average.

Mercer's team quickly tested a Liverpool defence that had conceded only 16 goals in 20 game but failed to get in a telling shot. Marshalled by Tommy Smith and Strong, the Reds were renowne for tough and uncompromising defending; although they were never dirty. Colin Bell, Mik Summerbee and Lee sustained injuries, but the Blues forwards were all quickly back in action.

Raising the tempo, Ian St John and Hunt both forced Ken Mulhearn into action. In a blood an thunder clash, Summerbee needed further treatment before Mulhearn brilliantly stopped a piledrive from St John whilst George Heslop twice saved the Blues as Liverpool pressed for a half-time lead.

Having shaded the opening period, Liverpool deservedly opened the scoring on fifty-one minute when Hunt tapped the ball into an unguarded net after Peter Thompson's superb cross evade Mulhearn before bouncing to the England star off a post. A goal behind, City suffered another blov in the sixty-fourth minute when Summerbee was forced to retire through injury, substitute Bobb Kennedy moving to right half and Mike Doyle joining the attack.

Kennedy was quickly into the action and, from his tidy clearance, the Blues hit back on seventy four minutes when Lee pounced on to a poor header by Emlyn Hughes before rounding Gerr Byrne and squeezing the ball past a despairing Lawrence. With the game on a knife-edge, th deadlock remained unbroken in spite of thrilling attacking play from both teams. Lacking Liverpool ruthlessness, City showed skill and creativity, repeatedly slicing through a rigid defence withou providing the telling finish their efforts deserved.

City forwards again received the accolades, but Alan Oakes and Doyle worked tirelessly i midfield whilst Heslop and Glyn Pardoe earned top ratings in defence. Unbeaten in 10 games, thes were exciting times for City supporters as the Blues remained in title contention.

Liverpool 1
Hunt

Manchester City 1
Lee

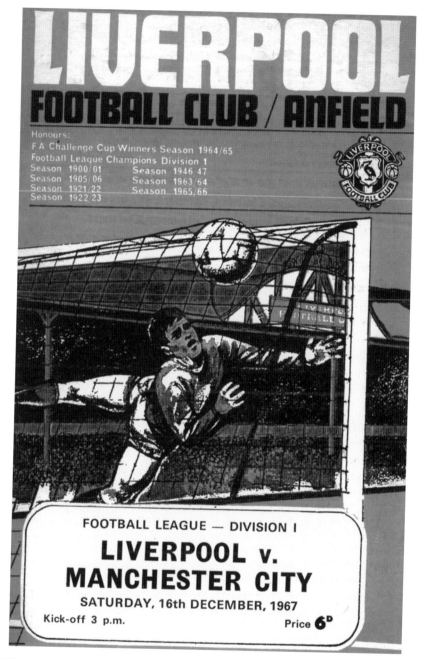

Liverpool: Lawrence, Lawler, Byrne, Smith, Strong, Hughes, Callaghan, Hunt, Hateley, St John, Thompson

Manchester City: Mulhearn, Book, Pardoe, Doyle, Heslop, Oakes, Lee, Bell, Summerbee (Kennedy), Young, Coleman

Manchester City v. Stoke City

Football League First Division **Date:** 23 December 1967 **Referee:** V. Batty (Helsby)
Location: Maine Road, Manchester **Attendance:** 40,121

Francis Lee provided City supporters with the perfect Christmas double as the Blues returned winning ways with a comfortable 4-2 triumph over Stoke City. City's sixth successive home victor and the fourth in which they have scored four or more goals, enabled Joe Mercer's team to aveng a 3-0 loss at the Victoria Ground in August, a result that saw City's boss switch Mike Summerbee centre forward.

Third-placed Blues were eleven games unbeaten after this win, two points adrift of Manchest United. Neil Young, Tony Coleman and Lee, with a brace, sealed City's win over Stoke, while e Blues star Peter Dobing and Harry Burrows were the opposition scorers.

Mercer selected an unchanged side from their classy 1-1 draw at Liverpool the previous wee Colin Bell and Summerbee had been on the treatment table and there were concerns over the fitne of Mike Doyle and Glyn Pardoe. All were able to start. Mid-table Stoke named the same team th had been a shade unfortunate to lose 1-0 at Arsenal.

Bell was in the wars with a shin injury inside five minutes but continued after lengthy treatmer Chances at both ends were kept out by excellent goalkeeping, Stoke stopper Gordon Banks particular showing his England class when saving brilliantly from Young.

Stoke took the lead on twenty-seven minutes after good work by Dobing and John Mahone Dobing having the easiest of tasks when faced with an unguarded net after Burrows' shot wɑ partially parried by Ken Mulhearn. City got back on level terms eight minutes later when Banl dropped a left-wing cross from Tony Coleman. Summerbee challenged for and won the loose ba before pulling it back for Young to hammer a low shot into the net. Taking control, City dominate to half-time and after the break Banks was quickly in action, saving brilliantly from Lee to mak amends for his earlier error.

The Blues continued to press forward and deservedly took the lead on sixty-five minutes, Le setting up Bell, before Tony Coleman fired home a loose ball off the underside of the crossba Sensing victory, both Lee and Summerbee went close before City extended their lead fourtee minutes from time when Summerbee held off a challenge from Alan Bloor before pulling the ba back for Lee to score with ease.

Standing between City and a goal bonanza, Banks was in superb form but English soccer's be goalkeeper could do nothing to stop Lee crashing home the Blues' fourth goal on eighty-nir minutes after pushing out a fierce cross from Coleman to the sharpshooter. In the final second Burrows scored a second for Stoke from a free-kick.

This was a comfortable win for the Blues, with Lee taking the accolades for a first-ra performance.

Manchester City 4	Stoke City 2
Young	Dobing
Lee (2)	Burrows
Coleman	

Manchester City: Mulhearn, Book, Pardoe, Doyle, Heslop, Oakes, Lee, Bell, Summerbee, Young, Coleman

Stoke City: Banks, Elder, Bentley (Bernard), Skeels, Bloor, Allen, Bridgewood, Mahoney, Dobing, Vernon, Burrows

WEST BROMWICH ALBION v. MANCHESTER CITY

Football League First Division   **Date:** 26 December 1967   **Referee:** R. Spittles (Great Yarmouth)
Location: The Hawthorns, Birmingham   **Attendance:** 45,074

High-flying City suffered severe Boxing Day blues with a first defeat in twelve games following an eighty-eighth minute strike by Jeff Astle. West Brom's striker scored twice in his club's 3-2 win in front of a capacity 45,074 crowd, taking Albion to the fringes of the top six whilst denting City's title aspirations. The Blues were still third but were now three points behind leaders Manchester United following the Reds' 2-2 draw at Leicester City.

City made three changes to the side that defeated Stoke City 4-2 three days before: Stan Bowles replaced the injured Colin Bell, Stan Horne came in for Mike Doyle and Roy Cheetham took the substitute's shirt. Seventh-placed Albion, who had drawn 0-0 against Southampton in their last game, included schemer Bobby Hope and prolific centre forward Astle in their starting line-up. Full-back Eddie Colquhoun, however, would not be facing his former Bury teammate Bell.

Encouraged by The Hawthorns' largest crowd for four seasons, Albion stunned Joe Mercer's team with a double blast in the first half. Astle struck first with a bullet header from a right-wing corner that City 'keeper Ken Mulhearn was unable to hold before wing half Tony Brown, a former Manchester Boys star, hammered in a second as Albion threatened to run away with the points. While the hosts were in control, City's forward line lacked penetration and, without the vision and skill of Bell, the snap and sparkle was missing.

Although outplayed and deservedly behind at half-time, the Blues bounced back on the hour through a spectacular strike by Francis Lee, and Mike Summerbee raised hopes of an unlikely win in the seventy-fourth minute when he slotted in an equaliser. The stage was set for a thrilling finish and the points looked like going City's way when a George Heslop header from a corner arrowed towards the Albion net; but John Osborne got his fingertips to it and Graham Williams scooped the ball off the line. With two minutes left on the clock, joy came for Albion and heartache for City when Astle beat Mulhearn to grab a late winner.

City's fightback had been magnificent, but sloppy defending in a pulsating game ultimately cost them a share of the spoils. Scorning their usual policy of tightly knit defence, City paid the penalty when Astle pounced. Nevertheless, the Blues had demonstrated a never-say-die attitude in a spirited comeback with Summerbee, Lee and Neil Young all playing leading roles. Stand-in Bowles was hardly in the game, but full marks went to Horne who tackled with vigour.

West Bromwich Albion 3	Manchester City 2
Astle (2)	Lee
Brown	Summerbee

West Bromwich Albion v. Manchester City

OFFICIAL **ALBION NEWS**

AND PROGRAMME

WEST BROMWICH ALBION FOOTBALL CLUB LIMITED

President Major H. Wilson Keys, MC, T D

Directors Mr J. W. Gaunt *Chairman* Mr T. W. Glidden *Vice-Chairman*

Mr L. Prichards Mr C. H. James Mr F. A. Millichip Mr T. H. Silk

Secretary Mr Alan Everiss *Manager* Mr G. A. Ashman

Ground The Hawthorns West Bromwich *Grams* 'Football West Bromwich' *Phone* 021-553 0095

Club Colours, Shirts—Navy Blue and White Stripes *Shorts*—White

Vol. 59 No. 22 (Copyright)   26th December, 1967

ALBION v MANCHESTER CITY

SIXPENCE ●

West Bromwich Albion: Osborne, Colquhoun, Williams, Brown, Talbut, Fraser, Krzywicki, Kaye, Astle, Hope, Clark (Lovett)

Manchester City: Mulhearn, Book, Pardoe, Horne, Heslop, Oakes, Lee, Bowles, Summerbee, Young, Coleman (Cheetham)

MANCHESTER CITY v. WEST BROMWICH ALBION

Football League First Division **Date:** 30 December 1967 **Referee:** H. Williams (Sheffield)
Location: Maine Road, Manchester **Attendance:** 45,754

Tony Brown's second goal against City in four days left the Blues reeling after back-to-back defeat Dick Krzywicki and Brown gave West Brom the distinction of becoming the first team to recor a 'double' over title-chasing City as the Blues dropped to fourth spot behind Manchester Unitec Liverpool and Leeds.

The 2-0 home defeat in front of a bumper holiday crowd of over 45,000 was not the response Jo Mercer was looking for after City's 3-2 defeat at the Hawthorns on Boxing Day. With Colin Bell sti sidelined, John Clay, making his League debut, came into the City side for Stan Bowles while Sta Horne continued to deputise for 'flu victim Mike Doyle against an unchanged Albion side.

Clearly fired up, City monopolised the opening exchanges with Clay quickly establishing himse but, for a fourth successive match, the Blues gave their opponents a goal start. The breakthroug came on nineteen minutes with a cleverly conceived goal instigated by Clive Clark and Bobb Hope, Krzywicki volleying the ball past the diving Ken Mulhearn. Under overcast skies and wit thunder and lightening rumbling overhead, City tried to hit back immediately but failed to make an impression on a resolute Albion defence. Tempers frayed and City skipper Tony Book had his nam taken for scything down Clark in midfield.

A goal behind at the interval, City pressurised Albion on the resumption but an uncompromisin defence remained steadfast, despite good approach work from Francis Lee, Neil Young and Mik Summerbee. Raising the tempo, more City pressure saw John Osborne in desperate action, bu Albion were determined to hang onto their lead no matter what tactics they employed.

Conceding a string of free-kicks, and utilising a ten-man defence, the Blues' frustration wa complete when Albion made the points safe with a second goal on eighty-seven minutes, Brow calmly beating Mulhearn for a well-taken goal.

Albion thoroughly deserved this victory and over two games had proved too strong for Cit looking the more clinical side. City again missed the drive and workrate of Bell and, without h presence, Lee and Summerbee fell short.

These were worrying times for the Blues boss, who would be well aware that his team could nc afford to lose a third successive League game and fall further behind the title pacesetters. As Ne Year approached City were five points behind Matt Busby's Manchester United – but there was sti a long way to go before the honours were handed out.

Manchester City 0	West Bromwich Albion 2
	Krzywicki
	Brown

MANCHESTER CITY v. WEST BROMWICH ALBION

Manchester City: Mulhearn, Book, Pardoe, Horne, Heslop, Oakes, Lee, Clay, Summerbee, Young, Coleman

West Bromwich Albion: Osborne, Colquhoun, Williams, Brown, Talbut, Fraser, Krzywicki, Kaye, Astle, Hope, Clark

Nottingham Forest v. Manchester City

Football League First Division
Location: City Ground, Nottingham

Date: 6 January 1968
Attendance: 39,581

Referee: A. Diamond
(Harlow New Town)

City returned to winning ways after two Christmas defeats with a comfortable three-goal triumph at Nottingham Forest. Neil Young, Mick Summerbee and Tony Coleman did the damage in a much improved display as Joe Mercer's team got their title campaign back on the road again.

Mercer delayed his team selection until the very last minute, giving Colin Bell every chance to prove his fitness following his absence from back-to-back defeats against improving West Bromwich Albion. Unfortunately, it wasn't to be for Bell, David Connor deputising instead. Mike Doyle returned after recovering from 'flu. City fans got the opportunity to see tenth-placed Forest's new £100,000 signing Jim Baxter. The hots, who had claimed a Christmas 'double' over Stoke City, also included teenager Colin Hall as a replacement for England centre forward Joe Baker, laid low with 'flu.

A supercharged start by City was followed by pressure from Forest, with Frank Wignall in particular prominent. However, Baxter blunders handed City the initiative with two quick-fire goals. The Blues opener came on thirty-six minutes when Baxter pushed a clearance straight to Young, who rounded Terry Hennessey to score with a shot that rocketed under diving Forest 'keeper Peter Grummitt. Four minutes later City increased their lead, Baxter again at fault, upending Connor after a dangerous cross from Summerbee. Referee Diamond had no hesitation in awarding a penalty that was duly converted by Coleman.

Forest hit back furiously before the break but City's defence, marshalled superbly by skipper Tony Book, held firm and they nearly went further ahead through Connor and a Francis Lee special. City continued their assault in the second half; Grummitt though was in fine form and kept out efforts from Summerbee, Lee and Young. With the Blues in control, Grummitt just managed to save a thirty-five-yard shot from Connor but then needed treatment after landing awkwardly. From the subsequent corner, Summerbee headed home to end the game as a contest. Before the game could resume Grummitt received further treatment before leaving the pitch clutching his arm to be replaced between the sticks by striker Wignall.

There was no stopping City now as they headed for their first 'double' of the season. Credit to Forest's stand-in 'keeper, Wignall pulled off superb saves from teammate Bobby McKinlay, who was guilty of a wayward back-pass, and an Alan Oakes header.

City emerged from the shadows of a Christmas nightmare with two priceless points but, more importantly, their confidence and workrate had returned. Although lucky to have been gifted two goals, the Blues tamed a talented Forest side. Young turned in a classy display, outshining Welsh international Hennessey. George Heslop was again imperious in defence and Doyle's return helped stabilise the midfield. Connor gave a solid performance and Summerbee never allowed Forest veteran defender Bob McKinley the opportunity to settle all afternoon.

Nottingham Forest 0	Manchester City 3
	Young
	Coleman
	Summerbee

Nottingham Forest v. Manchester City

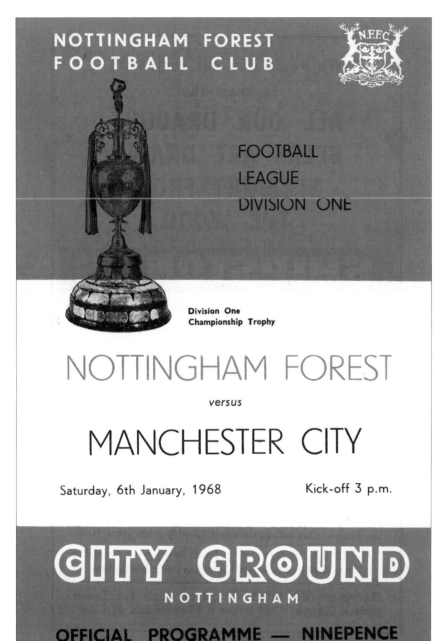

NOTTINGHAM FOREST FOOTBALL CLUB

FOOTBALL
LEAGUE
DIVISION ONE

Division One
Championship Trophy

NOTTINGHAM FOREST

versus

MANCHESTER CITY

Saturday, 6th January, 1968   Kick-off 3 p.m.

CITY GROUND
NOTTINGHAM

OFFICIAL PROGRAMME — NINEPENCE

Nottingham Forest: Grummitt (Taylor), Hindley, Winfield, Hennessey, McKinlay, Newton, Lyons, Baxter, Hall, Wignall, Hilley

Manchester City: Mulhearn, Book, Pardoe, Doyle, Heslop, Oakes, Lee, Connor, Summerbee, Young, Coleman

SHEFFIELD UNITED v. MANCHESTER CITY

Football League First Division
Location: Bramall Lane, Sheffield

Date: 20 January 1968
Attendance: 32,142

Referee: J. Yates (Redditch)

Colin Bell made a scoring return as the Blues notched up a second consecutive three-goal triump
Francis Lee and Mike Doyle completed City's second 'double' of the season, having hammered tl
Blades 5-2 in September. The result kept City in fourth spot, five points behind Manchester Unite
With Bell back after his ankle injury, City were able to field a full-strength side with David Conn
dropping to the bench. Blades, who had gained an impressive 1-1 draw at Arsenal the week befor
gave Pat Buckley, their new signing from Wolves, a home debut while a late change of referee sa
Mr Yates replace 'flu victim Mr Lyden.

In a feisty opening, both defences had to be on their guard and the referee was forced to cal
down several over-exuberant players before eventually booking Mike Summerbee. City slow
began to push the Blades back and appeared to have opened the scoring when Neil Young crashe
a shot against a post before the ball rolled gently into the net, only for the effort to be ruled out f
offside. With Willie Carlin looking lively, Sheffield enjoyed opportunities but the initiative swu
City's way on forty-one minutes when George Heslop fed Bell, who thundered home a twenty-fiv
yard screamer into the top corner.

Connor joined the action for the injured Tony Coleman after the interval. Undaunted, Sheffie
enjoyed plenty of possession and should have equalised on fifty-six minutes from the penalty sp
when Heslop upended Buckley, but Alan Woodward put his right-foot shot straight at Ken Mulhea
in the City goal.

With Buckley orchestrating play, the Blades put City under pressure but Mercer's side double
their advantage on seventy-five minutes when Lee made no mistake from a spot-kick after Bar
Wagstaff tackled Connor from behind in the penalty box. A third City goal looked on when Lee toe
a free-kick following a foul on Bell just outside the penalty area, but his shot struck the crossbar. Ci
finally scored their third on eighty-nine minutes when a long drive from Doyle thudded against tl
underside of the bar prior to bouncing over the line.

Back on track, there was no doubting the Blues' supremacy, especially in a first half when the
should have sewn up the match. City's defence had weathered the Blades' second-half storn
admittedly ungracefully at times, before victory was eventually secured with two late goals. Bel
return had given the team added power and drive while Alan Oakes and Doyle kept the midfie
powerhouse ticking over.

Sheffield United 0

Manchester City 3
Bell
Lee
Doyle

SHEFFIELD UNITED v. MANCHESTER CITY

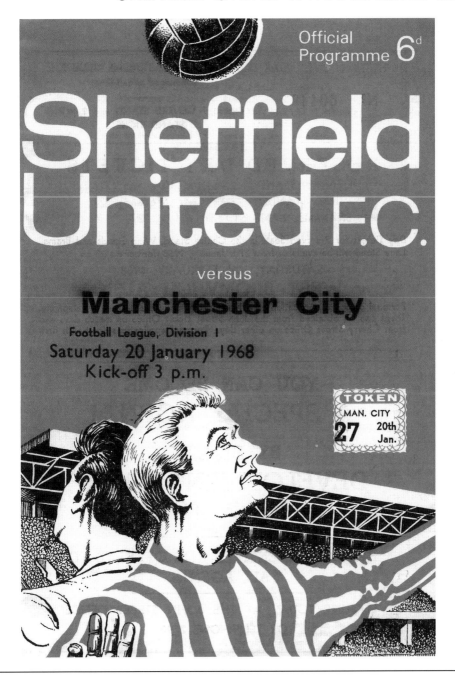

Sheffield United: Hodgkinson, Badger, Munks, Fenoughty, Mallender, Wagstaff, Woodward, Carlin, Hill, Addison, Buckley

Manchester City: Mulhearn, Book, Pardoe, Doyle, Heslop, Oakes, Lee, Bell, Summerbee, Young, Coleman (Connor)

MANCHESTER CITY v. ARSENAL

Football League First Division   **Date:** 3 February 1968   **Referee:** K. Howley (Middlesbrough)
Location: Maine Road, Manchester   **Attendance:** 42,392

A hotly disputed goal by Francis Lee earned the Blues a draw in an enthralling encounter at Maine Road. The 1-1 score was not the result Joe Mercer was looking for against mid-table Arsenal as City attempted to reverse a 1-0 defeat at Highbury in September. Fourth-placed Blues were now six points adrift of leaders Manchester United, although they did still have a match in hand.

City had followed their 3-0 victory over Sheffield United in their previous League game with a 7-0 mauling of Reading in a midweek FA Cup replay. Mercer named a full-strength side after Tony Coleman passed a late fitness test and George Heslop, Tony Book and Colin Bell shook off knocks. Arsenal, who had lost at Tottenham Hotspur in their last League match before scraping past Shrewsbury Town in the FA Cup after a replay, started with their £90,000 signing from Coventry City, Bobby Gould, in attack.

Taking the game to Arsenal, Terry Neill and Ian Ure blunted everything City threw at them in the opening fifteen minutes and what looked like a certain goal from a Bell overhead kick was brilliantly saved by Gunners 'keeper Jim Furnell. City continued to press Arsenal but failed to penetrate a resolute defence. On their rare excursions upfield, the League Cup finalists did create chances and Ken Mulhearn was forced into action to push a good effort by George Armstrong over the bar.

Goalless at the interval, City came out positively after the break. Lee was left thumping the ground in frustration after losing possession to Peter Storey when well placed before Heslop forced Furnell to drop the ball, but Neill cleared the danger. Neil Young crashed a right-foot shot against the body of Furnell when clean through and City were left rueing missed opportunities when Arsenal took the lead in the fiftieth minute.

John Radford started the move before Gould, with his first constructive pass of the match, found George Graham unmarked to beat Mulhearn from ten yards. Arsenal almost made it 2-0 a minute later when Heslop, attempting to clear, headed the ball against his own bar – Mulhearn made a flying dive to smother the rebound.

Undeterred, City came back into the game with a controversial goal on seventy minutes. Lee latched onto a Bell through-ball and lifted into the air a shot that dipped under the bar. As Coleman challenged Furnell, the ball bounced down before being cleared; however, to Arsenal's astonishment referee Howley indicated a goal, despite strong protests from the Gunners defenders.

Sensing an opportunity to grab both points, Mike Summerbee began to get the better of Ure. Young saw a tremendous drive strike the bar before having a goal chalked off, the referee ruling that the ball had gone out of play before Coleman crossed. With both teams going for the victory, Arsenal almost grabbed a win on the final whistle when Radford headed an Armstrong cross onto the City bar.

This was a deserved point for both sides when the Blues demonstrated their battling qualities against an Arsenal side determined to take home at least a share of the spoils.

Manchester City 1	Arsenal 1
Lee	Graham

Manchester City: Mulhearn, Book, Pardoe, Doyle, Heslop, Oakes, Lee, Bell, Summerbee, Young, Coleman

Arsenal: Furnell, Storey, Simpson, McLintock, Neill, Ure, Radford, Gould, Graham, Sammels, Armstrong

MANCHESTER CITY v. SUNDERLAND

Football League First Division   **Date:** 24 February 1968   **Referee:** H. Daly (Mansfield)
Location: Maine Road, Manchester   **Attendance:** 28,624

The Blues claimed a hard-fought win against a resolute Sunderland team courtesy of a clinical second-half strike by sharpshooter Francis Lee. Returning to League action after a three-week break, the win kept Joe Mercer's team in fourth spot, five points behind leaders Manchester United.

City, who had drawn 1-1 with Arsenal in their last League encounter before losing 4-3 to Leicester City in an FA Cup fourth-round replay (having been 2-0 ahead), faced a Sunderland team just three points clear of bottom-placed Fulham. City lined up without Mike Summerbee, who was making his England debut against Scotland at Hampden Park, and Neil Young, who was out with a gashed ankle. City brought in Chris Jones and David Connor, while Stan Bowles returned to the bench. Sunderland, who had lost 1-0 at home to Tottenham Hotspur last time out, included new £70,000 wing half Calvin Palmer.

Despite early pressure, City failed to break the deadlock with Sunderland conceding three corners in the first ten minutes. The Wearsiders tested the Blues' defence on a couple of occasions, but only Jim Montgomery in the Sunderland goal prevented Lee, Tony Coleman and Colin Bell from opening the scoring for the hosts. Sunderland had little to offer in attack and City 'keeper Ken Mulhearn was only called into action by the occasional thirty-yard back-pass. Nevertheless, the score remained goal-less at half-time.

On the resumption, Coleman had the ball in the Sunderland net but his effort was ruled offside. Constantly under pressure, Sunderland resorted to trips and body checks, which resulted in a series of free-kicks, but City failed to capitalise. With the game deadlocked, chances were rare but Coleman saw a spectacular airborne volley skim the bar while George Mulhall had a free shot kicked away by Mulhearn.

Class, however, had to tell and City's pressure finally paid dividends on seventy-three minutes when Lee, running brilliantly into space to accept an Alan Oakes pass in his stride on the right edge of the Sunderland goal, fired an angled shot past Montgomery. Despite the goal, City failed to add a second against Sunderland's eight-man defence. However, they had little difficulty claiming the points.

Undoubtedly, the Blues had missed the presence of Summerbee and Young, who would have provided extra power and penetration against an uncompromising Sunderland blockade. However, in freezing conditions, City's defence was hardly troubled. The disappointment of the cup knockout still lingered despite this triumph but Mercer would have been satisfied that fourth-placed City were in touch with the leaders, even if they remained six points adrift of neighbours Manchester United.

Manchester City 1   Sunderland 0
  Lee

Manchester City: Mulhearn, Book, Pardoe, Doyle, Heslop, Oakes, Lee, Bell, Jones, Connor, Coleman

Sunderland: Montgomery, Irwin, Ashurst, Todd, Kinnell, Palmer, Brand, Suggett, Harris, Harvey, Mulhall

BURNLEY v. MANCHESTER CITY

Football League First Division **Date:** 2 March 1968 **Referee:** C. Thomas (Rhondda Valley)
Location: Turf Moor, Manchester **Attendance:** 23,458

Francis Lee repaid another slice of his transfer fee with a second-half penalty to claim the points in an entertaining encounter at Turf Moor. With leaders Manchester United losing 3-1 at Chelsea, Lee's fourth strike in successive League games kept City in fourth place and reduced the gap at the top to four points.

Eleventh-placed Burnley, who lost 1-0 at Nottingham Forest the previous week, were looking to avenge a 4-2 defeat at Maine Road in November but became another of City's 'double' victims. Mike Summerbee's return from international duty and Neil Young's recovery from a badly gashed ankle enabled Joe Mercer to name a more balanced side than in their 1-0 win over Sunderland last Saturday. City ran out in all-white, watched by a large contingent of Blues supporters from three sides of the ground while the old stand was being rebuilt. The new stand was to be the first in Britain to incorporate under-floor heating – but the pitch was anything but state-of-the-art. In poor condition, it was mostly rolled mud and sand with little grass.

The game opened with City on the offensive but Burnley soon settled into slick, attractive football, putting City's defence on the back foot, and Ken Mulhearn had to be alert to keep the Clarets at bay. With Burnley showing better control and more direct passing, the Blues had several lucky escapes leading up to half-time, especially in the forty-first minute when striker Andy Lockhead fluffed a simple header from five yards with the goal gaping after Mulhearn failed to gather a Willie Morgan free-kick.

On the resumption City began to look more lively with Summerbee, Lee and Colin Bell particularly dangerous. Forcing several corners in quick succession, at last City were putting pressure on Harry Thomson in the Burnley goal and becoming more confident in attack. Despite appearing calm under pressure, Thomson slipped up on sixty-five minutes when he upended Bell as he raced through the Burnley defence. Lee converted the penalty with ease to break the deadlock. The game was now unrestrained with action at both ends and Dave Merrington was booked for a foul on Summerbee.

On seventy minutes City almost conceded from a Burnley corner when a Merrington header hit the post before being scrambled away by Blues skipper Tony Book but, counter-attacking, Lee played a good through-ball to a well-placed Colin Bell, but Bell slipped whilst shooting. Maintaining pressure, the Blues gained five corners in quick succession and the fifth nearly led to a second City goal when Mike Doyle's header hit the bar. A minute later Thomson pulled off a brilliant save at the second attempt to deny a Doyle drive.

Defeating their East Lancashire rivals, after defending for much of the first half, would have pleased Mercer, as City stayed in title contention.

Burnley 0   Manchester City 1
                                                    Lee

BURNLEY *v.* MANCHESTER CITY

Tony Book leads City out.

Burnley: Thomson, Ternent, Latcham, Todd, Waldron, Merrington, Morgan, Lockhead, Casper, O'Neill, Coates

Manchester City: Mulhearn, Book, Pardoe, Doyle, Heslop, Oakes, Lee, Bell, Summerbee, Young, Coleman

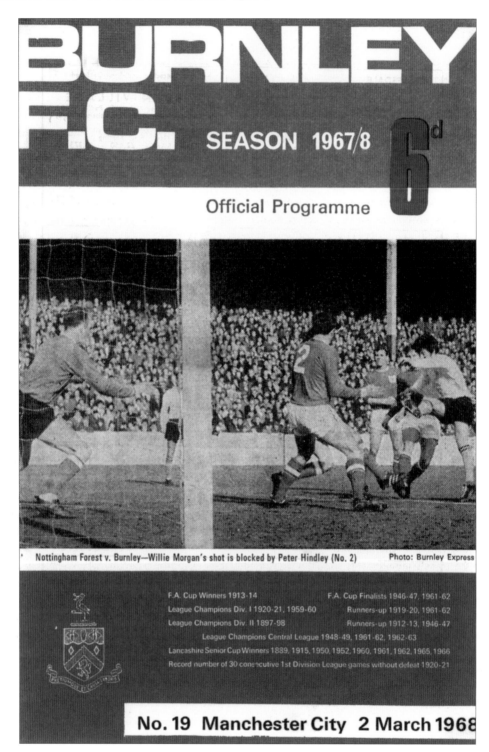

BURNLEY F.C.

SEASON 1967/8

6d

Official Programme

Nottingham Forest v. Burnley—Willie Morgan's shot is blocked by Peter Hindley (No. 2)   Photo: Burnley Express

F.A. Cup Winners 1913-14   F.A. Cup Finalists 1946-47, 1961-62
League Champions Div. I 1920-21, 1959-60   Runners-up 1919-20, 1961-62
League Champions Div. II 1897-98   Runners-up 1912-13, 1946-47
League Champions Central League 1948-49, 1961-62, 1962-63
Lancashire Senior Cup Winners 1889, 1915, 1950, 1952, 1960, 1961, 1962, 1965, 1966
Record number of 30 consecutive 1st Division League games without defeat 1920-21

No. 19 Manchester City 2 March 1968

Manchester City v. Coventry City

Football League First Division   **Date:** 9 March 1968   **Referee:** R. Tinkler (Boston)

Location: Maine Road, Manchester   **Attendance:** 33,310

The Blues' title charge remained on course after they scored three goals at home for the first time since December in an action-packed clash that saw two players sent off. Mike Summerbee, Colin Bell and Neil Young secured a third successive win, catapulting City into second spot with 41 points from 30 games, one ahead of Leeds United, who had a game in hand, and two behind leaders Manchester United.

Hoping for a goal bonanza against a Coventry team that had leaked 57 goals already this season, the Blues, looking to build on a 1-0 win at Burnley, fielded a full-strength team after Tony Book and Alan Oakes passed fitness tests. Coventry, beaten 3-1 at Everton on the previous Saturday, selected recent £90,000 signing striker Neil Martin and teenage star Willie Carr.

Both teams created early opportunities before City opened the scoring on eighteen minutes, Summerbee tapping home after Bell headed against the crossbar from a Coleman corner. Determined to increase their lead, City piled forward against a Coventry side that showed little finesse and seemed happy to employ cynical tactics – Summerbee needed treatment and Bell took time to recover from a vicious tackle by Maurice Setters before Bruck savagely chopped down Coleman. Following another flashpoint, referee Tinkler endured the wrath of City players when he refused to award a penalty after Summerbee was hacked down by John Tudor.

With tempers becoming frayed, three minutes before half-time, Coleman appeared to aim a kick at Bruck, resulting in Tinkler ordering both Coleman and Bruck off. Players from both teams jostled Tinkler, with even City's assistant manager Malcolm Allison joining in, as the half ended on a sour note.

The half-time interval enabled both teams to calm down and, four minutes after the resumption, City took a grip on the match with a fine goal. Moving the ball with speed from a Tony Book free-kick on the edge of City's six-yard box, Francis Lee, Bell and Mike Doyle put Summerbee in possession on the right, Bell rising superbly to head past Bill Glazier from Summerbee's pinpoint cross. City were now well on top but Coventry reduced the deficit in the seventy-seventh minute when Tudor squeezed the ball between Ken Mulhearn and the post. Any hopes of a comeback, though, vanished three minutes later when City restored their two-goal cushion following a right-wing corner, Bobby Kennedy setting up Young to fire home.

In the closing minutes, City should have extended their lead from a penalty when Setters hauled down Summerbee, but Glazier denied Lee with a superb double save. Despite the miss, Lee was still joint top First Division scorer, alongside West Ham and England star Geoff Hurst, with 23 goals.

City's class eventually told against a Coventry team whose dire position showed in their ruthless approach, but Mercer's charges were now chasing down their Old Trafford neighbours. Summerbee, Bell and Young all impressed, while George Heslop and Doyle kept a firm grip in defence.

Manchester City 3   **Coventry City 1**

Summerbee   Tudor

Bell

Young

MANCHESTER CITY v. COVENTRY CITY

Manchester City: Mulhearn, Book, Pardoe, Doyle, Heslop, Oakes (Kennedy), Lee, Bell, Summerbee, Young, Coleman

Coventry City: Glazier, Bruck, Clements, Machin, Setters, Tudor, Hannigan, Baker (Lewis), Martin, Carr, Rees

MANCHESTER CITY v. FULHAM

Football League First Division
Location: Maine Road, Manchester

Date: 16 March 1968
Attendance: 30,773

Referee: P. Baldwin
(Thornton-in-Cleveland)

The Blues led a compelling title race on goal average, following a thumping five-goal win against relegation favourites Fulham. Overcoming the shock of an early goal by Young England striker Allan Clarke, City came back to win a fourth consecutive match and top the table alongside Manchester United, who surprisingly lost 2-0 to struggling Coventry City. In a scintillating display, Neil Young with two, Mike Summerbee, Colin Bell and Francis Lee all scored for the Blues.

Making one change from last week's 3-1 win at Coventry, Bobby Kennedy replaced the injured Alan Oakes, who ended a run of sixty-eight consecutive League and cup appearances. Fulham, 2-0 victors against Sheffield Wednesday on the previous Saturday, included former England skipper Johnny Haynes in their team.

Despite being in control throughout the first half, City failed to exploit a ragged Fulham defence and allowed them to play a brand of football that belied their bottom-place standing. In the thirteenth minute City conceded a goal, Clarke collecting Haynes' defence-splitting pass and waltzing past George Heslop and Ken Mulhearn before pushing the ball into an empty net. Three minutes later City equalised when Mike Doyle slipped a ball to Bell, who looked offside but went on to hammer the ball into the roof of the Fulham net.

Taking control, City took the lead on twenty-five minutes when Summerbee broke away on the left and squared the ball to Young, who placed his left-foot shot wide of Ian Seymour. The Blues kept Fulham under pressure and were unlucky not to increase their lead on the stroke of half-time when Tony Coleman's fierce shot bounced back off the post. City scored a third goal in the sixty-third minute after Seymour brought down Summerbee for a penalty, Lee firing home the rebound after his initial shot was saved.

Despite Haynes' promptings, Fulham found it impossible to make inroads against a now-rampant City, who scored the game's best goal in the seventy-ninth minute when Kennedy pushed a fine pass through to Young, who brilliantly beat Reg Matthewson before crashing a shot past Seymour. Strolling now, the Blues sealed a fine win with a fifth goal of the afternoon on eighty-five minutes, Summerbee calmly beating Seymour after a superb pass by Lee.

City had played well within themselves against a plucky Fulham side, but once Bell had wiped out the Londoners' lead there was only going to be one winner. The big test would come with visits to championship rivals Leeds United and Manchester United in the space of four days. Only then would supporters know if Joe Mercer's team had the temperament to claim a first League title since 1937.

Manchester City 5

Bell   Summerbee
Young (2)
Lee

Fulham 1

Clarke

MANCHESTER CITY v. FULHAM

*Colin Bell, scorer of
City's first goal.*

Manchester City: Mulhearn, Book, Pardoe, Doyle, Heslop, Kennedy, Lee, Bell, Summerbee, Young, Coleman

Fulham: Seymour, Brown, Dempsey, Matthewson, Nichols, Conway, Haynes, Callaghan, Earle, Clarke, Barrett

CITY

VERSUS
FULHAM

SEASON
1967-68

MANCHESTER CITY F.C.
MAINE ROAD, MANCHESTER.
LEAGUE DIVISION 1 CHAMPIONSHIP.

SATURDAY, 16th MARCH 1968
Kick-off 3-0 p.m.

OFFICIAL PROGRAMME

1/-

LEEDS UNITED v. MANCHESTER CITY

Football League First Division **Date:** 23 March 1968   **Referee:** D. Lyden (Birmingham)
Location: Elland Road, Leeds **Attendance:** 51,818

Quadruple-chasing Leeds edged ahead in the battle for the First Division Championship with second-half goals from Johnny Giles and Jack Charlton. Their 2-0 win took them two points clear at the top of the table alongside Manchester United, while City dropped down to third spot. Undefeated at home this season, Leeds (who already had the League Cup tucked away in the trophy cabinet), extended their unbeaten run to twenty-two matches as they chased four major honours. Despite losing out, Joe Mercer's title contenders were, however still in the hunt with ten games remaining.

The Blues welcomed back Alan Oakes, Bobby Kennedy dropping to the bench. Leeds made one change from the side that had drawn 0-0 at Chelsea, Terry Hibbitt replacing Paul Madeley, who reverted to substitute.

In front of a near-capacity crowd of over 50,000 at Elland Road, both sides carved out chances in a blistering opening. City should have taken the lead on eighteen minutes when Mike Summerbee's astute pass sent Colin Bell clear, but Leeds 'keeper Gary Sprake brilliantly saved Bell's attempt to flick the ball past him. City were starting to dominate in a period that coincided with the absence of Leeds' skipper Billy Bremner, who had left the field with blood pouring from a head wound after a fifteenth-minute clash with Summerbee. Bremner was off the field for ten minutes and came back with several stitches over his left eye. His return saw Leeds put pressure on City and force Ken Mulhearn into some spectacular action. The teams went in level at half-time and showed the huge crowd why they were vying for top spot.

Leeds reshuffled their line-up in the second half, Madeley replacing Hibbitt, Peter Lorimer switching to right-wing and Jimmy Greenhoff moving to the left. Picking up the pace, Leeds took the lead on fifty-three minutes, Mick Jones threading Norman Hunter's pass between George Heslop and Oakes for Giles to beat Mulhearn with a low drive. Buoyed by the breakthrough, Leeds wrapped up the points with a second goal in the sixty-eighth minute after Heslop was penalised for pulling down Madeley just outside the City penalty area, Charlton heading home Giles' pinpoint cross from Bremner's quickly taken free-kick.

After the game, Mercer told his players that this defeat was not the end of their championship dream. City had played superb football in the first half and could have won this thriller before Giles and Charlton secured the victory for Leeds. Bell and Summerbee did all they could to inspire City but lacked support up front. Behind them, Alan Oakes turned in a magnificent display.

Dropping these points in the tightest title race for years left the Blues with little scope for further slips. Next up was the much-awaited derby clash against Manchester United at Maine Road. This was City's last match of the campaign to be televised by BBC television's *Match of the Day* programme.

Leeds United 2 **Manchester City 0**
Giles
Charlton

Nº 04716

LEEDS UNITED A.F.C TOKEN

MANCHESTER CITY 48 1967-1968

OFFICIAL PROGRAMME ONE SHILLING

VERSUS

MANCHESTER CITY

SATURDAY, 23rd MARCH, 1968   K.O. 3 p.m.

NEXT HOME MATCHES

TUESDAY, 26th MARCH,   K.O. 8.30 p.m.   *Fairs Cup*

GLASGOW RANGERS

Tele-recording from Glasgow

SATURDAY, 30th MARCH,   K.O. 3 p.m.   *F.A. Cup*

SHEFFIELD UNITED

Leeds United: Sprake, Reaney, Cooper, Bremner, Charlton, Hunter, Greenhoff, Lorimer, Jones, Giles, Hibbitt (Madeley)

Manchester City: Mulhearn, Book, Pardoe, Doyle, Heslop, Oakes, Lee, Bell, Summerbee, Young, Coleman

Manchester United v. Manchester City

Football League First Division   **Date:** 27 March 1968   **Referee:** D. Smith (Stonehouse)
Location: Old Trafford, Manchester   **Attendance:** 63,400

The Blues were back in the title race following one of the greatest derby victories ever. Overcoming a thirty-eighth-second goal by George Best, strikes by Colin Bell, George Heslop and a Francis Lee penalty earned City a thrilling win. In reality, Joe Mercer's team was a class apart, playing with panache and professionalism, destroying United by a greater margin than the scoreline suggested. The result saw City join Leeds United and Manchester United in a three-way tie at the top of the table.

City named an unchanged side for this most critical of fixtures after a 2-0 defeat at rivals Leeds United. Matt Busby initially named the same team that had beaten Nottingham Forest 2-0 in their last outing, also adding Denis Law and Tony Dunne to the squad. Law had not played since United's victory at Arsenal in February, but was eventually named in the starting line-up.

United started as favourites and opened the scoring inside a minute when Best forced an error from Tony Book before shooting past Ken Mulhearn. City fans feared another derby beating as their team struggled after a shattering opening, but gradually the Blues gained midfield control and began to dictate the game. Although Mike Doyle was winning vital midfield tackles, Bell was United's main tormenter. Covering acres of ground with his running, chasing and harrying, his scintillating performance must have impressed England manager Alf Ramsey. United's defence was under severe pressure and eventually cracked when Bell deservedly scored an equaliser on fifteen minutes, blasting home an unstoppable shot past Alex Stepney.

Keeping up the pressure, City came out strongly in the second half and eventually scored the decisive second goal in the fifty-seventh minute, Tony Coleman curling a free-kick into the United penalty area for Heslop to head firmly past Stepney. Fighting back, United went close to scoring several times but this was to be City's night and, with the hosts pushing forward frantically, it was inevitable that Mercer's charges would get an opportunity to exploit space. Eventually an opportunity arose when Bell raced clear in the dying minutes, only to be scythed down by Francis Burns for a penalty. Following treatment, Bell was worryingly stretchered from the pitch with a nasty-looking injury before Lee stepped forward to fire his spot-kick past Stepney with aplomb and seal a well-deserved victory.

It was the night when Mercer cried with joy. Assistant Malcolm Allison summed the game up as a climax of three years' hard work, because a City side had never reached such heights of brilliance in his view. Bell's display was breathtaking and Heslop, who scored his first ever League goal for the Blues, was a colossus in defence. Doyle helped turn the tide for City but, on a magical night for the blue half of Manchester, every City player was magnificent.

Manchester United 1	Manchester City 3
Best	Bell
	Heslop
	Lee

rancis Lee goes close against Manchester United.

Manchester United: Stepney, Brennan, Burns, Crerand, Sadler, Stiles, Fitzpatrick, Law, Charlton, Best, Herd (Aston)

Manchester City: Mulhearn, Book, Pardoe, Doyle, Heslop, Oakes, Lee, Bell (Connor), Summerbee, Young, Coleman

LEICESTER CITY v. MANCHESTER CITY

Football League First Division   **Date:** 6 April 1968   **Referee:** H. New (Farlington)

Location: Filbert Street, Leicester   **Attendance:** 24,925

The Blues endured a black day in their League Championship quest with struggling Leicester City claiming victory courtesy of a Mike Stringfellow second-half strike. After the euphoria of last week's win over Manchester United, Joe Mercer's title pretenders were expected to claim victory over the Midlanders; instead they allowed rivals Leeds United to leap back into top spot after defeating Sheffield United 3-0, with Manchester United losing 2-1 at home to Liverpool. City were now in third spot with 45 points, ahead of Liverpool on goal average. Both teams were two points adrift of the top two but, in the closest title race in years, with eight games remaining, the championship was still anybody's.

City made one change, David Connor replacing the injured Colin Bell. Leicester, who drew 0-0 at Newcastle United in midweek, included Dave Gibson – who had starred in the Foxes' FA Cup fourth-round 4-2 victory over City in February.

In a scrappy opening, Leicester edged the early skirmishes but both sides found it difficult to make headway with a near stalemate in midfield. City, missing the influence of Bell, allowed Leicester far too much freedom in the centre and only poor finishing and good goalkeeping from Ken Mulhearn prevented Leicester from taking the lead. Gradually though, the Blues imposed themselves and, on the stroke of half-time, Tony Coleman had a great chance to put City ahead from six yards, but failed to make contact with a superb Francis Lee cross.

Seconds after the restart Leicester scored with a splendid goal, Gibson cutting the ball back for Stringfellow to plant it firmly past Mulhearn. With Gibson the creative spark, only solid defending prevented Leicester scoring a second goal and killing off the game. Francis Lee was the only City forward to display any real thrust in what was turning out to be a lacklustre performance. Neil Young, Mike Summerbee and Connor all proved ineffective in front of goal and, with time running out, City were becoming desperate for an equaliser. However, a lack of penetration enabled Peter Shilton to remain virtually untroubled.

Despite a better second-half display, the Blues never looked like getting a goal in a poor showing. One man doesn't make a team, but Bell's return from injury could not come soon enough for Mercer and his team's title aspirations. Certainly, the Blues boss looked on in dismay at Filbert Street knowing that one of his star players could end up missing most of the remaining fixtures. These were worrying days at Maine Road.

Leicester City 1   Manchester City 0
Stringfellow

LEICESTER CITY *v.* MANCHESTER CITY

George Heslop on the ball.

Leicester City: Shilton, Rodrigues, Bell, Roberts, Sjoberg, Cross, Tewley, Nish, Large, Gibson, Stringfellow

Manchester City: Mulhearn, Book, Pardoe, Doyle, Heslop, Oakes, Lee, Connor, Summerbee, Young, Coleman

Leicester
City
FOOTBALL CLUB

SEASON 1967-1968
FOOTBALL LEAGUE DIVISION 1
AT FILBERT STREET, LEICESTER

MANCHESTER
CITY
SATURDAY 6 APRIL 1968

OFFICIAL PROGRAMME **6**d

MANCHESTER CITY v. CHELSEA

Football League First Division   **Date:** 12 April 1968   **Referee:** J. Taylor (Wolverhampton)
Location: Maine Road, Manchester   **Attendance:** 47,132

City's championship challenge was back on track following a smash-and-grab triumph at Maine Road. Playing the first of two home Easter fixtures in twenty-four hours, Mick Doyle notched his fifth strike of the season to earn Joe Mercer's team a crucial victory after the disappointment of their recent loss at Leicester City. Next up were West Ham United, then a trip to Chelsea in three days' time. With Leeds United losing 2-1 at Tottenham Hotspur, Manchester United thumping Fulham 4-0 and Liverpool losing 2-1 at home to lowly Sheffield United, Mercer's title pretenders were back up to third spot and firmly in the mix.

Due to Colin Bell's continued absence, City made one change, Bobby Kennedy replacing David Connor for his second start of the campaign. Chelsea named the same XI that had drawn 2-2 at Sheffield Wednesday the week before.

The opening exchanges saw no quarter given by either side. Francis Lee, Mike Summerbee and Neil Young endeavoured to find openings for City, while Peter Osgood and Alan Birchenall foraged away in attack for the opposition. With Chelsea threatening danger from both flanks through the silky skills of Charlie Cooke and Peter Houseman, City's Tony Book and Glynn Pardoe had to be on their toes at all times. Although Lee and Osgood went close with a couple of strikes, in general both defences, marshalled by Alan Oakes and David Webb, were limiting opportunities in a nip-and-tuck encounter. It was clear that one goal could prove crucial and, with so much at stake for City, there was relief all round for Mercer, Malcolm Allison and the Blues' supporters when Doyle was on hand to knock a priceless goal past Peter Bonetti. Despite constant pressure from the Londoners, through commitment and desire City claimed two precious points to keep their title bandwagon on the road.

This was a fine win for the Blues. After the frustration at Filbert Street, questions had been asked of whether the City players had the mental toughness to last the pace. The answer came resoundingly through this victory against an uncompromising outfit brimful of talent.

Unquestionably, the season was going to the wire and there were to be more twists and turns during the run-in, but one thing in City's favour was that they would have no fixture congestion. In addition to crucial League matches, Leeds United had FA Cup and Fairs Cup-ties to negotiate, while Manchester United had European Cup battles ahead of them. With City ahead of Liverpool, there looked to be no better opportunity for Mercer's charges to claim English football's top domestic honour.

Manchester City 1   Chelsea 0
  Doyle

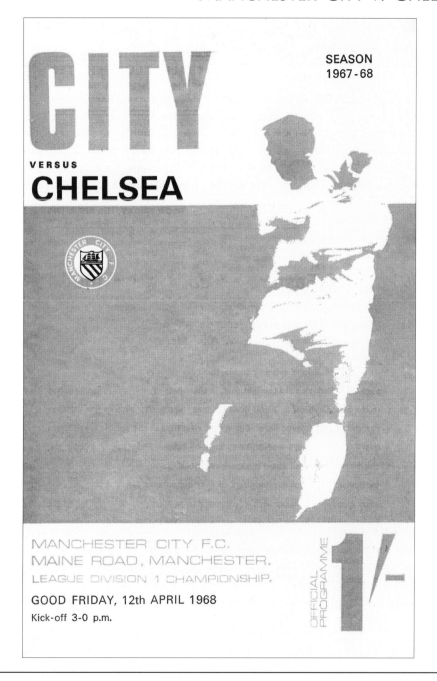

Manchester City: Mulhearn, Book, Pardoe, Kennedy, Heslop, Oakes, Lee, Doyle, Summerbee, Young, Coleman

Chelsea: Bonetti, Harris, Thomson, Webb, Hinton, Cooke, Baldwin, Osgood, Birchenall (Fascione), Houseman

MANCHESTER CITY v. WEST HAM UNITED

Football League First Division   **Date:** 13 April 1968   **Referee:** M. Fussey (Retford)
Location: Maine Road, Manchester   **Attendance:** 38, 755

A brilliant brace by Neil Young hammered home City's title credentials as the Blues made it an East doubIe for ecstatic supporters. For the second time in two days, City took on London opposition an finished victorious, following up a 1-0 win against Chelsea on Good Friday with this 3-0 rom against West Ham to make themselves the only top-four team to take full points from the Easte programme. Mike Doyle was also on the scoresheet for the second game in a row. With leade Manchester United drawing at Southampton, third-placed City closed the gap to just one point the title race.

Bobby Kennedy replaced Doyle at right half, Doyle moving up front to take Colin Bell's number shirt. West Ham, 3-0 victors over Nottingham Forest the day before, included World Cup trio Bobl Moore, Martin Peters and Geoff Hurst in their starting line-up.

City were quick off the mark from the opening whistle but missed two glorious chances early on. the sixth minute Young sliced his shot wide after good work by Mike Summerbee, then Summerbe himself failed to make contact with a pass from Francis Lee that split the Hammers defence and le goalkeeper Bobby Ferguson totally exposed.

Creating chances at will, Tony Coleman somehow blazed over from inside the six-yard box. A go had to come and City's pressure finally paid off in the eleventh minute. Moore blocked Colemar right-wing centre but City's winger crossed the rebound into the middle for Young to volley hom left-footed past Bobby Ferguson's reach.

A goal ahead, the Blues inadvertently allowed West Ham back into the game with Moore promptir his strikers. George Heslop was dominant in the City defence and virtually single handedly kept tl Hammers at bay. Gradually, though, City came back into the game after a lengthy period under tl cosh, but failed to double their lead before half-time when Summerbee and Lee somehow contrive to miss golden opportunities.

On the resumption, no doubt pepped up by a stern team talk, Ferguson was again in actio saving in quick succession from Summerbee and Lee. Under siege, when Billy Bonds was unable clear a Coleman overhead kick, Ferguson was powerless to prevent a second City goal on fifty-tw minutes, Lee collecting the loose ball for Young to smash into the net for his second of the match.

In complete control, Ferguson turned a Lee drive behind for a corner and, keeping up the pressur City counter-attacked from a West Ham corner to score in the fifty-seventh minute when, after goc work by Coleman and Summerbee, Doyle delivered the killer blow with a powerful header past bemused Ferguson.

West Ham, apart from a good spell before the interval, were never a serious threat and left Mair Road indebted to their brave stopper for keeping the score down. Heslop again stole the limelig

Manchester City 3   **West Ham United 0**
  Young (2)
  Doyle

... s City's most consistent defender, while Kennedy slotted into the team neatly. Mercer though would
... e keenly awaiting medical reports on Bell as destiny beckoned in the final six games.

... anchester City: Mulhearn, Book, Pardoe, Kennedy, Heslop, Oakes, Lee, Doyle, Summerbee, Young, Coleman

... est Ham United: Ferguson, Bonds, Lampard, Peters, Stephenson, Moore, Redknapp, Boyce, Brooking (Charles), Dear, Hurst

CHELSEA v. MANCHESTER CITY

Football League Firsrt Division   **Date:** 16 April 1968   **Referee:** W. Gow (Swansea)
Location: Stamford Bridge, London   **Attendance:** 36,466

High-flying City's title aspirations took a hammer blow at Stamford Bridge following a predatory strike by Chelsea sharpshooter Alan Birchenall. Joe Mercer's championship pretenders were going for a third consecutive Easter win, having defeated Chelsea 1-0 and West Ham 3-0 without conceding a goal. However, in an engrossing encounter, Mercer's charges did everything but score. Some days are kind; some days are cruel. This was a day when the team deserving to win did not get their just rewards. City remained in third spot, two points behind Leeds United and three adrift of Manchester United, 3-0 winners over Fulham – though both sides had a match in hand on the leaders.

Prior to the match, City received news that Tony Coleman had been given a seven-day suspension for his sending-off against Coventry City in March, along with Coventry's Dietmar Bruck. Minus Coleman, Mercer solved his selection problems by bringing back Bobby Kennedy. Kennedy played when City beat Fulham in the previous month and his slotting in at right half enabled Mike Doyle to continue, in Colin Bell's continuing absence, at inside right. Chelsea, 2-0 derby winners over Tottenham Hotspur the previous Saturday, made one change from the side beaten 1-0 at Maine Road on Good Friday, Eddie McCreadie returning in place of Jim Thomson.

Dominating from the start, only a blanket defence in front of 'keeper Peter Bonetti saved Chelsea from falling behind, Francis Lee, Mike Summerbee and Neil Young all going close in the opening period.

The second half followed a similar path with City playing some of their most dazzling football of the season but, for all their efforts, they could not breach a Chelsea defence employing at times nine men in front of Bonetti. Biding their time, and against the run of play, Birchenall snapped up the winner for Chelsea.

The very least City deserved from this one-way clash was a point. How they lost was beyond belief with George Heslop, Alan Oakes and Kennedy all having sound games in defence and joining the attack to harass a Chelsea rearguard, which steadfastly refused to crack.

The defeat left City rank outsiders to take Manchester United's title, but Mercer's charges would continue to battle to the end. They now faced a trip to Wolves, who were fighting to stay out of the relegation zone.

Chelsea 1   **Manchester City 0**
   Birchenall

CHELSEA FOOTBALL CLUB

STAMFORD BRIDGE GROUNDS London SW6

LEAGUE DIVISION 1
SEASON 1967-68

Tuesday, 16th April

v

MANCHESTER CITY

Kick-off 7.30 p.m.

OFFICIAL **1/-** PROGRAMME

LEAGUE CHAMPIONS 1954-55   LEAGUE CUP WINNERS 1964-65

Chelsea: Bonetti, Harris, Thomson, Hollins, Webb, Hinton, Cooke, Baldwin, Osgood, Birchenall, Houseman

Manchester City: Mulhearn, Book, Pardoe, Kennedy, Heslop, Oakes, Lee, Doyle, Summerbee, Young, Connor

WOLVERHAMPTON WANDERERS v. MANCHESTER CITY

Football League First Division   **Date:** 20 April 1968   **Referee:** H. Davies (Cardiff)
Location: Molineux, Wolverhampton   **Attendance:** 39,622

City's title hopes were slipping away fast following a dour 0-0 draw at Molineux that did neither side any favours. The Blues' one-goal midweek defeat at Chelsea appeared to have exhausted the number of points they could possibly spare in the scramble for the title. Now Joe Mercer's side were really up against it if they were to retain any interest in the championship race. With Manchester United defeating Sheffield United 1-0, Leeds United beating Tottenham Hotspur 1-0 and overcoming West Brom 3-1, only Liverpool's 3-1 defeat at West Ham did City any favours. Leeds were one point behind the League leaders but still had a match in hand, while the Blues had a game in hand but were now four points adrift of their Old Trafford rivals. Liverpool were six points adrift with two games in hand.

Speaking to journalists afterwards, Joe Mercer conceded that City's hopes of claiming the title were fading after dropping three points in five days. Mathematically, the Blues could still lift the First Division crown, but it was no longer in their hands. They needed rivals to slip up.

The return of Colin Bell was seen as a good omen for City, although it did create selection problems for Mercer with David Connor having played so well against Chelsea in Tony Coleman's absence through suspension. In the end, Bobby Kennedy dropped to the bench, Mike Doyle reverting to right half to accommodate Bell in attack. Wolves, just two points above the relegation zone after a 2-0 defeat at Sunderland, had ex-City favourite David Wagstaffe in their side alongside Derek Dougan.

Wolves kept the Blues' defence at full stretch in a first half that saw Ken Mulhearn by far the busier of the two goalkeepers. Finding it hard to get into the game, City's best effort came on thirty-nine minutes when Neil Young had Parkes at full stretch, the Wolves 'keeper only just managing to push the ball behind for a corner. With both sides desperate for points, the first half was uninspiring, most of the action confined to a grim midfield tactical battle.

In no mood to give anything away, the second half degenerated into mounting frustration for City. Both sides squandered gilt-edged chances, Frank Wignall blasting wide from ten yards with only Mulhearn to beat before Summerbee did likewise nine minutes from time.

The irony for City was that they played badly and secured a point, while they had lost against Chelsea when turning in a top-class display. On his return from injury, Bell had lacked the imagination that made City's front line one of the most feared in the League. George Heslop had an intriguing battle with Dougan but overall this was a poor match.

Wolverhampton Wanderers 0   Manchester City 0

WOLVERHAMPTON WANDERERS v. MANCHESTER CITY

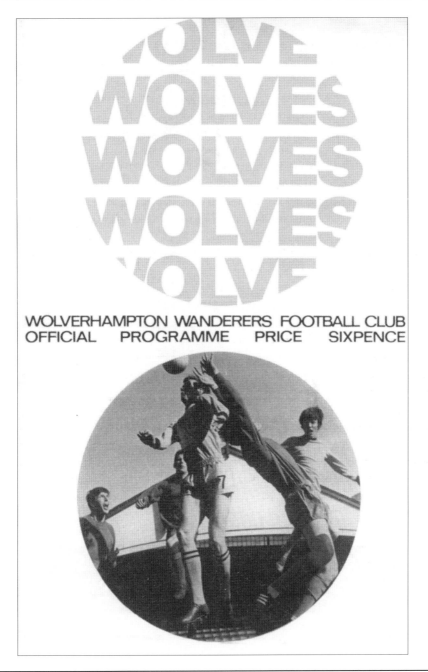

Wolverhampton Wanderers: Parkes, Parkin, Thomson, Bailey, Woodfield, Holsgrove, Kenning, Wignall, Dougan, Knowles, Wagstaffe

Manchester City: Mulhearn, Book, Pardoe, Doyle, Heslop, Oakes, Lee, Bell, Summerbee, Young, Connor

MANCHESTER CITY v. SHEFFIELD WEDNESDAY

Football League First Division **Date:** 25 April 1968 **Referee:** D. Corbett (Essington)
Location: Maine Road, Manchester **Attendance:** 32,999

The Blues' jittery championship challenge was back on track with three matches remaining courtesy of a freak own goal by Owls forward Brian Usher and outrageous luck in this 'must-win' game in hand over League leaders Manchester United. City's good fortune came in an unconvincing display that saw Wednesday denied a blatant penalty and a last-minute goal direct from a David Ford corner. Referee Corbett's failure to spot either incident left City hanging onto the coat tails of both Manchester United and Leeds United, who lost 3-2 at Stoke City. The Blues were now a point behind Leeds and just two points adrift of Matt Busby's star-studded side. All three sides had now played thirty-nine games. Liverpool had two matches in hand but were four points behind City.

The Blues took a short break in Southport before entertaining Wednesday and Joe Mercer took the opportunity to tell his players that, despite the disappointing 0-0 draw at Wolves last Saturday, securing the title was still entirely in their hands. City were back at full strength, with Tony Coleman returning after suspension. Alan Oakes was playing his 300th League game for City in a game played, unusually, on a Thursday night. Mid-table Owls, who drew against Nottingham Forest last time out, made one change, Usher replacing Johnny Fantham on the right flank. The Blues, without a goal in two games, faced a Wednesday side who were also finding goals hard to come by, having scored only three times in their last five League games, a run that had placed them dangerously close to the relegation zone.

Taking the game to Wednesday, City had numerous opportunities to seal the match. Given the freedom of the park by the Owls' static defence in the first half, Francis Lee, Colin Bell and Coleman all inexplicably failed to take full advantage, much to the frustration of the home supporters. A game in which a hatful of goals were there for City to take was eventually decided on forty-three minutes, Usher, under pressure from Lee, deflecting Neil Young's indirect free-kick beyond Peter Springett into his own net. Undaunted, Wednesday fought back and left the field fuming when the referee ruled out not only a penalty, after Book hacked down Ritchie on the penalty spot, but also a late goal when Ford's corner appeared to cross the line before Ken Mulhearn scooped it to safety. City players admitted later that the ball had crossed the line but it was too late for the Owls, who left Maine Road empty-handed.

Next up are Everton and a clash with the FA Cup finalists.

Manchester City 1   **Sheffield Wednesday 0**
  Usher (o.g.)

SEASON 1967-68

CITY

VERSUS

SHEFFIELD WEDNESDAY

MANCHESTER CITY F.C.
MAINE ROAD, MANCHESTER.
LEAGUE DIVISION 1 CHAMPIONSHIP.

THURSDAY, 25th APRIL 1968

Kick-off 7-30 p.m.

OFFICIAL PROGRAMME **1/-**

Manchester City: Mulhearn, Book, Pardoe, Doyle, Heslop, Oakes, Lee, Bell, Summerbee, Young, Coleman

Sheffield Wednesday: Springett, Smith, Megson, Young, Mobley, Eustace, Usher, McCalliog, Ritchie, Ford, Woodall

Manchester City v. Everton

Football League First Division **Date:** 29 April 1968 **Referee:** F. Wallace (Swindon)
Location: Maine Road, Manchester **Attendance:** 37,776

The title race was going down to the wire following a comfortable 2-0 victory for the Blues against Everton, with Joe Mercer's title pretenders leading the way on goal average. Second-half goals against the FA Cup finalists by Tony Book, his first of the League campaign, and Tony Coleman, brought a crucial win for City, catapulting them into top spot following Manchester United's 6-3 thumping at West Brom the previous Saturday. Mercer's team headed the field on 54 points alongside their Old Trafford neighbours. Liverpool were still in the hunt after a 4-1 win over Fulham, but Leeds United would pinch the title if they won their remaining three matches. Don Revie's team were one point behind City and United, but had a match in hand following their FA Cup semi-final defeat to Everton at the weekend. This was only the second time that City had led the table in this most compelling of seasons, the previous occasion lasting a week following a 5-1 romp against Fulham in March.

For City's last home game of the season, Mercer named a full-strength side while Everton manager Harry Catterick refused to rest his star players – despite their cup exertions.

Knowing a win was vital, City started the match cautiously and only picked up a pedestrian performance after half-time following news from the Hawthorns that Manchester United were sensationally down by two goals. United's possible demise generated an electric atmosphere within Maine Road and provided the launching pad for a whirlwind second-half display that left Everton demoralised by the ferocity of City's forward line. Rising to the occasion, City's playmakers, subdued in recent games, began a siege of Gordon West's goal. The Blues' opener came from the most unlikely source, skipper Book emerging from a penalty area melee to smash the ball past West. For Book, the goal was ample compensation for his penalty miss on the opening day against Everton's Merseyside neighbours Liverpool.

Everton had battled hard but their task was made more difficult when, having already replaced Tommy Jackson with substitute Jimmy Husband, they were forced to see out the game with ten men after midfielder Howard Kendall left the field with concussion.

Nothing was going to stop the now-rampant Blues and, taking full advantage, Colin Bell took control of the game to give his best display since he destroyed Manchester United with a virtuoso performance during the previous month. Coleman was not far behind and scored City's second, his ninth of the season, with a tremendous shot that West could not hold and which dropped over the line. Everton almost grabbed a consolation goal when Joe Royle smashed a drive onto the underside of the City bar but, this was not to be the young striker's or his side's day as the Blues claimed a vital win.

The 2-0 result did not do justice to a dazzling second-half performance by City, who signed off their home campaign in thrilling fashion. In one of the tightest races for years, if City were to claim the title, they would still have to do it the hard way. First, they needed Leeds to lose one or

Manchester City 2 Everton 0
  Book
  Coleman

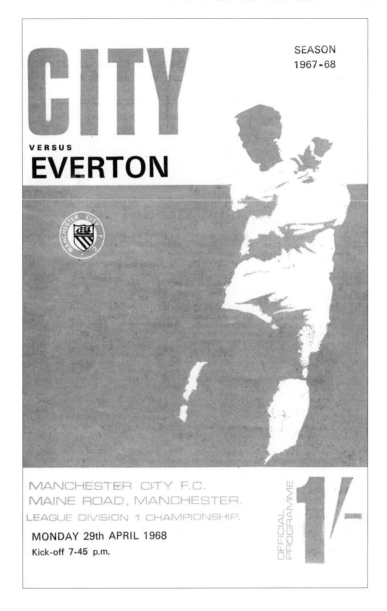

more games and then they faced away trips to Tottenham Hotspur and Newcastle United, while Manchester United had home fixtures against Newcastle United and Sunderland. Two victories would clinch the title on goal average.

Manchester City: Mulhearn, Book, Pardoe, Doyle, Heslop, Oakes, Lee, Bell, Summerbee, Young, Coleman

Everton: West, Wright, Wilson, Kendall, Labone, Harvey, Husband (Jackson), Ball, Royle, Hurst, Morrissey

TOTTENHAM HOTSPUR v. MANCHESTER CITY

Football League First Division   **Date:** 4 May 1968   **Referee:** L. Callaghan (Glamorgan)
Location: White Hart Lane, London   **Attendance:** 51,242

The Blues were one victory from the First Division title following a thrilling 3-1 victory at White Hart Lane. Two superb goals from Colin Bell and a third by Mike Summerbee settled a pulsating match as Joe Mercer's championship pretenders closed in on the ultimate honour in English football. In one of the tightest championship battles for years, City and United both had 56 points but the Blues were ahead on goal average. They would have to win at Newcastle United to claim the crown for the first time in thirty-one years. Manchester United, who defeated Newcastle 6-0, needed the Blues to slip up to wrest the title away from their neighbours. Leeds United and Liverpool each had 53 points with a game in hand after the Merseysiders won 2-1 at Elland Road. Both were now rank outsiders, needing to win their remaining fixtures while hoping the Manchester teams would each lose their last game.

Naming the same XI for a third match running, City needed to win against a free-wheeling Tottenham Hotspur side that had drawn 1-1 at Liverpool in midweek. The Blues started with confidence, probing for a breakthrough. Early chances fell to Mike Doyle, Neil Young, Tony Coleman and Francis Lee, but City couldn't get the breakthrough. Likewise, sixth-placed Tottenham created openings through Alan Gilzean, Martin Chivers and Jimmy Greaves, which George Heslop coped with admirably.

In the fortieth minute, City's finesse paid dividends after neat interplay between Tony Book, Coleman and Summerbee, Bell waltzing around Dave Mackay before gliding the ball past Pat Jennings in the Tottenham goal. Shell-shocked Tottenham were indebted to Jennings for a brilliant save within thirty seconds to deny Young but, seconds into the second half, City doubled their advantage, Bell hammering the ball through a crowd of defenders past Jennings after Cyril Knowles had initially cleared Young's snapshot off the line. Tottenham were far from finished but City's defence stood firm and, in the seventy-fourth minute, they grabbed a third goal, Bell linking with Lee to create an opening for Summerbee to slice the ball home.

To their credit, Tottenham continued to press forward and reduced the deficit seven minutes from time after a City defender handled a Jimmy Greaves free kick. Greaves made no mistake from the spot. Before the finish, City should have scored a fourth following a Mackay gaffe, but Lee blazed the ball over when a goal seemed certain, and on the final whistle Young clipped the bar with Jennings beaten.

Missed opportunities aside, City's performance was breathtaking. Tottenham's open style of play suited Mercer's team and the result was a match worthy of winning the title itself. Once the Blues had established a two-goal lead, they played tight at the back with Heslop, Book and Glynn Pardoe all looking unbeatable. One player stood out, however – Bell, fit again, turned in an outstanding performance.

City remained second favourites for the title behind Manchester United according to bookmakers. However, the Blues still fancied their chances of securing the required win.

Tottenham Hotspur 1   **Manchester City 3**
Greaves (pen)   Bell (2)
   Summerbee

Tottenham Hotspur *v.* Manchester City

Glyn Pardoe in action.

Tottenham Hotspur: Jennings, Beal, Knowles, Mullery, England, Mackay, Robertson, Greaves, Chivers, Venables, Gilzean

Manchester City: Mulhearn, Book, Pardoe, Doyle, Heslop, Oakes, Lee, Bell, Summerbee, Young, Coleman

Official Programme

Price **SIXPENCE**

TOTTENHAM HOTSPUR

v.

MANCHESTER CITY

FOOTBALL LEAGUE—DIVISION ONE

Saturday, 4th May, 1968

KICK-OFF 3 p.m.

SEASON 1967–68

Vol. 60 No. 51

Newcastle United v. Manchester City

Football League First Division   **Date:** 11 May 1968   **Referee:** J. Thacker (Scarborough)
Location: St James' Park, Newcastle   **Attendance:** 46,300

Now it was over – City had done it! On a day of thrilling football, Manchester City clinched the First Division crown. Thrills and spills, seven goals, end-to-end excitement, a capacity crowd, there could be no finer way of achieving the ultimate domestic prize than this sensational football match at St James' Park. City won 4-3 with goals from Mike Summerbee, Neil Young (2) and Francis Lee, wrapping up the title for the second time in their history, the last being in 1937. The Blues would now play in Europe for the first time.

It had taken manager Joe Mercer and assistant Malcolm Allison three years to transform City, one of football's aristocrats, from a mediocre Second Division outfit to Football League Champions and they deserved all the accolades that were to come their way.

On the final day of one of the tightest championship battles for years, the Blues knew a win would settle the title irrespective of scores elsewhere and they delivered in dazzling style. Leeds United's midweek defeat at Arsenal ended their slim hopes, while only if both Manchester City and Manchester United lost could Liverpool have had any chance of the championship.

Colin Bell and Summerbee had pulled out of England's midweek match against Spain to make sure they would be fit. Mercer, thrilled with City's sensational 3-1 win at Tottenham Hotspur last week, named the same eleven for a fourth consecutive game. Tenth-placed Newcastle United, thumped 6-0 by Manchester United the week before, made several changes. Skipper Jim Iley returned along with John McNamee, while in attack Bryan 'Pop' Robson replaced David Elliot, who dropped to the bench. Nearly 20,000 City supporters made the trip to Tyneside, swelling the crowd to 46,300.

Tensions were high as an electric atmosphere enveloped the terraces prior to kick-off and the early exchanges set the tone for an afternoon of unbridled excitement. City grabbed the initiative with the opening goal on thirteen minutes, after a clash between Summerbee and McNamee had brought a 'calm-it-down' lecture from referee Thacker. From the free-kick, Mike Doyle combined with Bell before sending in a superbly flighted near-post ball that Summerbee raced in to hit past Ian McFaul. The Blues' joy, however, was short lived, with Newcastle wiping out the lead inside ninety seconds, 'Pop' Robson hammering home a Jackie Sinclair diagonal ball past Ken Mulhearn.

Losing some self-belief, City allowed Newcastle more of the game but got back on track after thirty-two minutes when Young cracked the ball gloriously past McFaul from the edge of the penalty area. Yet again though, in this see-saw game, Newcastle came back strongly, Iley knocking George Heslop's loose clearance into the middle for Sinclair to shoot spectacularly past Mulhearn. Young had the ball in the net two minutes before half-time but his effort was ruled offside as a pulsating forty-five minutes finished 2-2.

Newcastle United 3	Manchester City 4
B. Robson	Summerbee
Sinclair	Young (2)
McNamee	Lee

NEWCASTLE UNITED *v.* MANCHESTER CITY

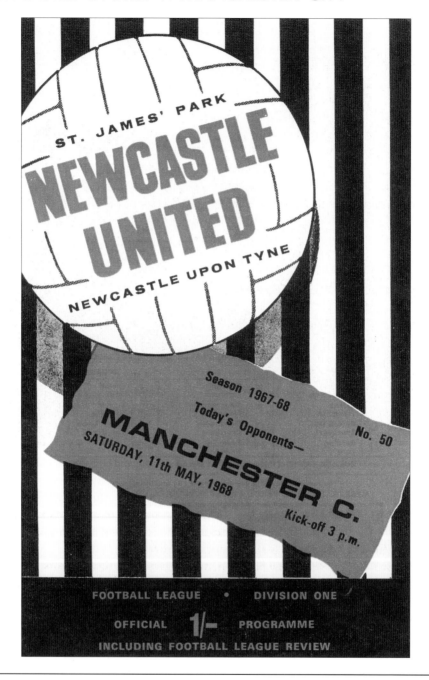

Newcastle United: McFaul, Craig, Clark, Moncur, McNamee, Iley, Sinclair, Scott, Davies, B. Robson, T. Robson

Manchester City: Mulhearn, Book, Pardoe, Doyle, Heslop, Oakes, Lee, Bell, Summerbee, Young, Coleman

Summerbee opens the scoring against Newcastle.

No doubt pepped up by Mercer and Allison, within four minutes of the restart City had their noses in front again. McFaul parried Bell's shot into the path of the onrushing Young, who made no mistake with another superb goal, his twenty-first of the season.

Playing with style and composure, on fifty-seven minutes Lee appeared to score the Blues' fourth goal only to see it ruled out by the referee, who waved away City protests. Seven minutes later, though, City did go further ahead, Bell slicing open Newcastle's offside trap for Lee to delicately chip the ball over the advancing McFaul. Ecstatic Blues supporters now sensed that they were at long last supporting the Champions.

Newcastle, to their credit, refused to concede defeat and, four minutes from time, in one final twist to a quite remarkable game, McNamee firmly headed 'Pop' Robson's spectacular right-wing cross past a stunned Mulhearn. City, however, were not to be denied and at the final whistle thousands of euphoric supporters invaded the pitch to acclaim their heroes, chanting 'Champions, Champions'. As City's victorious team made a dash for the changing rooms, skipper Tony Book, Young and George Heslop were hauled shoulder-high by jubilant City fans and it took dozens

NEWCASTLE UNITED v. MANCHESTER CITY

Francis Lee seals the title with City's fourth.

of policeman to get through delirious fans. Eventually, the players made it to the sanctuary of the dressing room to begin celebrations

Capping a remarkable day, news came through that Sunderland had surprisingly defeated Manchester United to give City a final margin of two clear points. So sure had the media been that United would beat Sunderland and City would fall at the final hurdle that *Match of the Day* featured highlights of the United v. Sunderland clash! Manchester City supporters though were not complaining; they were now finally acclaiming the First Division Champions.

Afterword

Commenting immediately after the final game in the Saturday evening 'Football Pink' (*Manchester Evening News & Chronicle*), Albert Alexander, the Manchester City chairman, commented:
Yes, Joe's right, this is the happiest moment of my football life. I'm also pleased for the sake of our directors; this is a just reward for their selection of Joe Mercer as manager, the players, management, backroom staff and the loyal fans who have stood by us in bad times as well as good.

City players mob goalscorer Lee.

City fans celebrate their team's title-clinching win at Newcastle on the St James' Park pitch.

AFTERWORD

Joe Mercer said:

This is so pleasing to me, but I'm particularly happy for the chairman. All his life he has bee devoted to City and this is a wonderful moment for him. It also sees us emerge from the shadow (United, which has been cast over Maine Road for so long.

Malcolm Allison added:

Europe here we come. I must compliment our fans. What a joy it brings us to see the blue, whi and maroon scarves wherever we go in this country. Let's hope they will follow us throughout th world. The title, the hardest football trophy to win in the world, is the reward of consistent hard wor by all the staff.

Tony Book noted:

We have put a lot into this season and because of this we thoroughly deserve the title. Wha will surprise many people, however, is that we have really enjoyed our football in these toug competitive days.

The paper's sports editor, Vernon Addison, penned an article entitled 'Salute this Swinging City':

Soccer's swinging City has hit the top note in playing the Rebirth of the Blues. Champions of th Football League. Sounds good doesn't it? You could set it to music. For the way Manchester City hav regained their self-respect is one of the great fightbacks of British sport. Three years ago City, one c the aristocrats of football's history, had, as has often happened to the English nobility, fallen on har times. They were on their uppers in the First Division with gates going as low as 8,015. Now the march into Europe like royalty. For this transformation praise the team, praise managers Joe Merce and Malcolm Allison, who go down as one of the great double acts of our time. But stop for a momen on this momentous day to praise a grey-haired grandfather, Albert Alexander, chairman of the Blues Mr Alexander took his whack of criticism as this great club was allowed to be run down. Then, three years ago, the directors decided to appoint their sixth post-war manager and generally get with it.

The board still irritated their faithful fans by taking an interminably long time over the appointment But, give them credit, when they came up with Joe Mercer, the former England wing half of th spindly legs and outstanding ability, they chose well. And Joe, in turn, picked well when he chose a his assistant Malcolm Allison, who could hardly be more different in temperament. Joe is studiou and quiet. Malcolm is vociferous, volatile and demonstrative. They have, however one thing i common: THEY KNOW WHERE THEY ARE GOING IN FOOTBALL.

But their journey has not been speeded by an ever-open cheque book. They have had to spen carefully, but they have spent wisely. Such fees as £45,000 for Colin Bell, £35,000 for Mike Summerbee, £17,000 for Tony Book, £25,000 for George Heslop, £12,000 for Tony Coleman and an equivalent of £25,000 for Ken Mulhearn are all bargains. And even the record fee of £60,00(for Francis Lee looks cheap at today's market prices. All these, and local discoveries too, have beer welded into one unit, a team in a true sense of the word. Yet, in these days of 'The Method' there i. still room for individual flair like Bell.

Well played, the entire City club both on the field and behind the scenes. For this is a popula and well-deserved success. What a wonderful day for their fans who have had to suffer, albeit wit

Lovely bubbly: City players celebrate in the dressing room.

great humour, the slings and arrows of United followers so long. Now Manchester is a united city, the number one footballing city in the world with United in the semi-finals of the European Cup and City top of England.

Strike up the band... the rebirth of the Blues followed by Alexander's ragtime band. That's my kind of swing.

In addition to Peter Gardner's comprehensive match report, the 'Football Pink' overviewed City's achievement in an article entitled 'Verdict on City':

Champions! Champions! We are the Champions! The gigantic, ear-splitting crescendo of sound rolled from the crammed Newcastle terraces to shatter the Tyneside air. Thousands of them had made the pilgrimage to be in on the great tower of glory and their joy spilled over as a truly magnificent City romped to victory, earning the two points that bridges a thirty-one-year gap by bringing the League title back to Maine Road.

It was, indeed, a match of truly great moments as City twice took the lead only to have it taken from them, but this was their big day and they had the steam, the power, the strength and skill to come back the more. Defensive mistakes gave Newcastle their two goals but Neil Young, the club's leading scorer this season, hit two fine shots, while Francis Lee and Mike Summerbee also got in on the act, but this was essentially a team performance. Top marks to Newcastle for making this a title decider to remember.

George Heslop and Colin Bell relax after the game.

Journalists nationally were euphoric about the new Champions.

Peter Gardner, 'Football Pink':
What a magnificent match to decide the title! What a tremendous climax to a magnificent season as Manchester City waged a thrilling battle with Newcastle United in a game fit to grace Wembley itself at St James's Park.

James Mossop, *Sunday Express*:
There could be no more popular, sentimental success story. City are – were – the poor relations of the Manchester clubs. Three years ago, discontented fans were throwing stones and abuse at the boardroom windows. The crowds had dwindled to a starvation level of 8,000. But in an amazing spell of hard work and dedication Joe Mercer and Malcolm Allison have lifted ordinary players into the Champions of the Football League. They are just a grand set of lads, mostly young, and the best all-round team in England. It is desperately difficult not to get emotional about Manchester City, about such a major success born out of honesty, bravery and complete dedication. This victory was the pinnacle of the season. An afternoon coloured with skill, blessed with fair play and above all applauded in the end by every man, woman, and child in the 50,000 crowd. These people will never forget it. Many thousands of them swarmed on to the pitch in a dancing, swirling sea of blue and white at the end. They were cheering for the new Champions. For ninety minutes City, the team that has won more friends than any other in a season of imaginative attacking football, turned on the style.

Vince Wilson, *Sunday Mirror*:
They were magnificent. A blue lightning speed outfit refusing to change the mood, which spelled only victory. If the ideal Championship winner exists at all, then this is it. It was City's Championship. They did it in wonderful style.

Eric Cooper, *Daily Express*:
It was this effort by Newcastle, exceeding in skill and efficiency most of their victories this season, that made the superb merit of City's triumph all the more glorious. In such an atmosphere of fast, open football and fierce tension, mistakes were excusable, but City were never less than Champions.

Ronald Crowther, *Daily Mail*:
The important thing about being Champions is to look like Champions. And sure enough, Manchester City strode home past the winning post at Newcastle with all the flair and conviction of footballers for whom this final issue was never in doubt.

Frank McGhee, *Daily Mirror*:
Even in the final match when tension was almost tangible and caution understandable Manchester City found the courage and confidence to go forward attacking.

John Bean, *Daily Sketch*:
In a race, which has taken every minute of nine months to run, Mercer's men have shown they have the guts, energy and skill to become Maine Road's first Champions since 1937.

Peter Gardner, *Manchester Evening News*:
All soccer has saluted Mercer, Allison and the City Buccaneers, and by golly, they deserve to drain every last drop of champagne from their glasses, for if anyone deserves a supreme accolade it is this bunch of one-time misses who have at last got a hit on their hands.

Eric Todd, *The Guardian*:
If they play attacking football as they have done these past months whatever the state of the game, then they will be welcomed and acclaimed wherever they go.

The Blues' journey back to Manchester was a long celebration as supporters surrounded the team bus to cheer the Champions home. Joe Mercer orchestrated singing; Malcolm Allison danced in the slow moving traffic. Queues formed on all the routes to Manchester.

The following day, City held a press conference at Maine Road, where Mercer, Allison and Book discussed City's success. With the Blues scheduled to embark on a close-season tour of America, a friendly against Bury was arranged for the Tuesday night following the Newcastle game to enable Mercer, Book & Co. to formally receive the First Division Championship trophy. City won 4-2.

Mulhearne, Young, Lee, Doyle and Oakes show off the championship trophy for the City faithful.

Manchester City players and management brought out a brochure celebrating the club's achievement, entitled *We are the Champions!* Containing articles on the players and their recollections of the season, Joe Mercer, in an article entitled 'Now City Will Become Even Better', noted:

Yes, we are the Champions. I am convinced my ears will never stop ringing with the shouts of acclaim and praise, which have been showered down on us all at Maine Road. And I will probably still be trying to reply to the masses of mail received from well-wishers when the events of 1968/69 have overtaken most memories.

All summer long, we have soaked ourselves with the glow of success, which our boys richly earned. We have unearthed a formula, no, better to say, the ingredients for success. There has to be fitness, ability and willingness to play as a side. Then, with all humility, you have got to have the breaks.

It happened for us last season. Since I am now a firm believer in modern-day miracles I feel that the best may yet be to come. For First Division Championships were beyond my wildest dreams when the task of leading this imposing Maine Road club was accepted by myself slightly over three years ago.

The painful part of success in football is that the enjoyment is so fleeting. The pace produces fresh challenges and new Everests to be scaled even before the inscription can be engraved on the medals from [the] last combat.

This title has given us new responsibilities. We are now exposed to other pressures. All summer long, I preached one message to the players: We have every right to be proud, I have told them. You're entitled to wear medals if you win them. The success gives people responsibilities. Pride of performance has always been professionals' motivating power rather than the money. Now we can become even better providing our attitude is right. We have not got the divine right to go out and win simply because we are the country's new Champions.

We have a small playing staff, and there were many times last season when some lads played and they should not have done so because of the injuries they suffered. They were helped in their decisions to carry on because of youth and enthusiasm and their appearance in the nation's sporting headlines was all new to them.

We learned some lessons rather severely last season. There was no actual turning point in winning the League. We played without anticipating winning the Championship, we had a lot of pride about our displays as a team, and we knew that on our day we could lick the best anywhere. The lads were playing in a way they enjoyed.

Our most important game was, quite obviously, the finale at Newcastle. The lessons learned revealed themselves. For my proudest match memory, I would probably choose the game at Spurs, which pitched us back into the Championship fray in a very big way. We could have gone from 3-0 to 8-0, the lads were that good.

There is one fact, which has constantly nagged supporters, and possibly the officials and players. The fact that we have been known as 'the other side in Manchester'. We can't hide from cold statistics and must accept the greatness Manchester United have achieved in post-war years. The worst thing that could happen to any of us is for traces of jealousy to show. Jealousy is dangerous to thinking and planning. Better to try and emulate, or improve on, United's past efforts. Let them heed me that there is no inferiority complex these days at Maine Road. I know that we can no longer be classed as Manchester's 'other team'.

Players commented on the Blues' triumph.

Colin Bell:
The output of effort is something we are proud of and it is there even in the most desperate situations. The lads never give up, even when they are behind. We are at our best when the pressure is on and the pressure was on during the last half of the season. I am proud to play with lads like this.

Tony Book:
I have never met a bunch of players who were so keen to do well. We worked hard last season in training, but I must say the training was enjoyable. These lads are good professionals.

AFTERWORD

Tony Coleman:
The lads worked hard and deserve everything they have got. We play the most attractive football in the First Division when we are allowed to play. The determination in the team is fantastic; this team never knows when it is beaten.

David Connor:
Teamwork and attacking football were responsible. The players have no doubt about their own ability. Anything Malcolm says the lads will do. If you respect the people in charge then you will always do things for them.

Mick Doyle:
We've played more consistently than anyone else. I think we did it without luck as well. Everyone works for everyone else and there is good team spirit. It was worth winning the title for big Malc and the boss.

Ken Mulhearn:
Our teamwork has been so consistent, even from when I first came early in the season it continued to improve. Everyone pulls for one another. When somebody has a bad game, the others rally round. Looking from the back, you get a picture of how they help one another. The only time we slipped up was when the forwards didn't help the defence in the cup game at Leicester, but look at the Spurs match – we kept going until they dropped.

Alan Oakes:
We are a great side and we have all worked hard. Most clubs expected us to crack and nobody thought we were capable of winning the title. We're the underdogs who have bitten hard at everybody. Even if we hadn't won the League we would have had a marvellous season.

Glyn Pardoe:
We have been made to believe in ourselves. We've come out and attacked teams, always going for goal. Everything stems from our training. It's so enjoyable. The boss and Malcolm have given us confidence to do things and without doubt the match at Manchester United proved finally to all fair-minded judges that we had a valid claim for the title.

Neil Young:
We are the fittest side in the country. We lasted the season better than anyone else and grew in confidence. We murdered sides in the last twenty minutes when they had given their lot against us. Apart from the short absence of Colin Bell, we have been lucky with injuries, and this has helped. When you lose more than one player, it can affect the pattern of the team's play. The turning point was our win at Old Trafford.

Players recalled a favourite League match.

Colin Bell, Manchester United (away):
Can't forget it. That was the first time I've ever been carried off on a stretcher. We got a penalty for the last-minute foul on me. It was another foul on me that won us the free-kick for the second goal and I netted the first, the equaliser. I thought it was easy to play against United because they seemed poor defenders on this occasion. When Mick Doyle's cross came over for my goal, I felt Fitzpatrick should have got it away before I ran through. I didn't feel too good when that went in the net because the linesman had flagged and at first I thought it would be disallowed for some unfathomable reason. It wasn't.

Tony Book, Manchester United (away):
Apart from the mistake in the first minute, which cost a goal, I felt I played well. I realised I had slipped and allowed Best in for the goal, but I seemed to forget that boob straight away and the next pass I played was okay. When there were two or three minutes to go, on the far side of the field from the trainer's bench, I had eight touches of the ball without them getting near as we kept possession.

Mike Doyle, Liverpool (away):
I thought everything I did, I did quite well. I marked Roger Hunt, and the job didn't provide me with any anxieties. Then I nearly had the winner, breaking through in the very last minute and cracking a shot, which hit their 'keeper, Tommy Lawrence. It bounced out to Francis Lee, but caught him on the knee and went past the post as he shot. I also went to centre forward near the end of the match, I felt the Liverpool defence was very slow, with Tommy Smith covering everything for them.

George Heslop, Chelsea (home):
This match was really the start of a good run for the team, and it came in the last lap of the season. I just could not do anything wrong in the whole match and this is what games are all about. I felt better after that for a long time, though I remember the match at Manchester United as the best for the team. Against Chelsea, I was handling Peter Osgood and on this day, he was very uneasy, and there was plenty of help around me. The Easter games were good for me, bringing out some of my best ever form.

Bobby Kennedy, West Ham (home):
After playing a long while in the reserves I was beginning to doubt my own fitness, but being called in for three games in four days at Easter gave me the chance to prove a point, at least to myself. This Saturday match was the highlight for me. I was out to show them at the club that I have always believed in myself being ready to play. I felt I had a good game the previous day against Chelsea, and this one delighted me because of the way I was able to stand up to another ninety minutes so quickly. The last time I had played against West Ham we were winning 3-0 and lost 5-3. This was revenge in splendid style and after Easter I had no doubts at all about my fitness.

AFTERWORD

Francis Lee, West Ham (away):
I scored the best volley I have ever hit. Tony Book smacked it over fully forty yards from the right wing and I let fly from almost twenty-five yards out. It was perfect contact and the ball screamed in for the first of my two goals. I practise those volley shots regularly, but have never connected so perfectly before in a proper match. It was only my sixth League game for the team and a great booster for confidence. I was quite pleased with the second goal I scored too.

Ken Mulhearn, Sunderland (away):
It was the game after my debut against Manchester United. I was feeling pretty low because of a home defeat in my first match, but though we lost in this one as well, I did well enough to lift my confidence. Their right-winger scored the only goal; it swerved in off the far post. One incident I was proud of was when one of City's former players, Ralph Brand, broke through on its own and his shot deflected after hitting me. He shot again and I caught it, I was very pleased with that one.

Alan Oakes, Leicester City (home):
Everything seemed to go well, and I scored the first goal from pretty close in, taking it from an angle. Leicester were struggling, they play defensive soccer and I had more freedom to come forward than I had in all the other games. After playing for some time at the back with George (Heslop), this was a chance to be allowed so much room to press up. I can't recall anything going wrong and we paralysed them.

Glyn Pardoe, Chelsea (home):
The night before this match I was at home with a temperature of 102 and feeling very rough. I hardly slept through the night either. Yet when I got on the pitch, I didn't feel too bad, despite getting a knock on the mouth in the first half as well. Running about helped a lot, and I surprised myself with the way I coped with such a rotten preparation for the game.

Mike Summerbee, Nottingham Forest (home):
I got great satisfaction out of this performance. The Forest centre half, McKinlay, has always been known as a good defender, and yet he didn't do anything which restricted me. I notched a header, one of my specials from three yards range. I was lying at the far post to meet a cross Colin Bell and it didn't need a lot of planting in.

Neil Young, Tottenham Hotspur (home):
We didn't think the game was going to be played when we viewed the ice-bound pitch beforehand. It was bad, and I think conditions like this make players very aware of injury risks, but it was different when we got out there, we skated it, in every sense of the word. We were prepared to be bold and play, and on the treacherous top, they didn't seem able to get near enough to tackle. I had great freedom and, though my preference is for a wet ground, this surface proved ideal. I scored one as well when the 'keeper could only push out a right-wing corner. The team were in top mood throughout.

Football League First Division 1967/68 Final League Table

First Division	P	W	D	L	F	A	Pts
Manchester City	42	26	6	10	86	43	58
Manchester United	42	24	8	10	89	55	56
Liverpool	42	22	11	9	71	40	55
Leeds United	42	22	9	11	71	41	53
Everton	42	23	6	13	67	40	52
Chelsea	42	18	12	12	62	68	48
Tottenham Hotspur	42	19	9	14	70	59	47
West Bromwich Albion	42	17	12	13	75	62	46
Arsenal	42	17	10	15	60	56	44
Newcastle United	42	13	15	14	54	67	41
Nottingham Forest	42	14	11	17	52	64	39
West Ham United	42	14	10	18	73	69	38
Leicester City	42	13	12	17	64	69	38
Burnley	42	14	10	18	64	71	38
Sunderland	42	13	11	18	51	61	37
Southampton	42	13	11	18	66	83	37
Wolves	42	14	8	20	66	75	36
Stoke City	42	14	7	21	50	73	35
Sheffield Wednesday	42	11	12	19	51	63	34
Coventry City	42	9	15	18	51	71	33
Sheffield United	42	11	10	21	49	70	32
Fulham	42	10	7	25	56	98	27

Player and management profiles

Joe Mercer, manager: Began a distinguished playing career as a wing half at Everton in 1932. Tactically astute, Mercer won a First Division Championship medal in 1938/39 before joining Arsenal in 1947 having won 5 England caps and 26 wartime caps. At Highbury, Mercer won two First Division titles and an FA Cup winners' medal. After a brief spell as Sheffield United manager, Mercer guided Aston Villa to Second Division promotion and the League Cup. In 1965 Mercer became Manchester City manager. The Blues' most successful boss, Mercer, in tandem with Malcolm Allison, guided City to First Division, Second Division, FA Cup, League Cup, European Cup-Winners' Cup and Charity Shield successes. Coventry City general manger from 1972 to 1981, Mercer was also caretaker-manager for England in 1977.

Malcolm Allison, coach: With his playing career cut short at West Ham United in 1958 through illness, Allison turned to coaching. He worked with Cambridge University, Toronto and Plymouth Argyle before joining Joe Mercer as assistant and coach in 1965. He played an integral role in City's triumphs throughout their most successful era. 'Big Mal' went on to manage and coach numerous club, including two brief managerial spells at City in the 1970s.

Ken Mulhearn, goalkeeper: An athletic and reliable goalkeeper who joined City in September 1967 from Stockport County, with whom he had won a Fourth Division title, for £25,000. He made his Blues debut in the Manchester derby and kept his place for the remainder of the Championship-winning campaign, keeping 12 clean sheets. Mulhearn played 61 games for City, gaining a First Division winners' medal. 1967/68 appearances: 33.

Harry Dowd, goalkeeper: Played during the early part of the Championship season when City gained five consecutive wins, before losing his place to Ken Mulhearn. Blues' number one from 1962/63, Dowd, a key member of the Second Division title team, returned to the fray in 1968/69 when he won an FA Cup winners' medal. In twelve years at Maine Road, Dowd made 219 appearances, scoring one goal against Bury in 1964. 1967/68 appearances: 7.

Tony Book, full-back: Book made his top-flight debut at twenty-nine following a transfer from Plymouth Argyle in July 1966. Quick, decisive, and an inspirational leader, Book was the only ever-present in City's Championship season. City skipper during the club's glory years, Book claimed First Division, FA Cup, League Cup and European Cup-Winners' Cup honours. Voted joint Footballer of the Year with Dave Mackay in 1968/69, Book played 312 (3) games for City, scoring 5 times. Book managed City 1974-1979, guiding them to their most recent major honour, the 1976 League Cup. 1967/68 appearances: 42. Goals: 1.

lyn Pardoe, full-back: City's youngest debutant established himself in the first team in 1965/66. A olid tackler and excellent passer of the ball, he missed only one game in the 1967/68 campaign nd was the only regular outfield player not to score during the season. Pardoe played in every osition except goalkeeper and centre half during fifteen seasons at the club, winning First Division, econd Division, FA Cup, League Cup, and European Cup-Winners' Cup honours. Pardoe made 78 (2) appearances for City, scoring 23 goals, most memorably the Blues' winner in the 1970 eague Cup final. Pardoe returned as youth team coach. 1967/68 appearances: 41.

Mick Doyle, wing half: Joined City in 1962. Came through the youth system and established himself s a midfielder and defender, becoming a regular in 1965/66. A determined performer, Doyle was ne of the club's most consistent players throughout the Championship season, scoring vital goals gainst Chelsea and West Ham during the Easter period to keep City in contention for the title. Third n the all-time City appearances list, Doyle won First Division, Second Division, FA Cup, League up (2) and European Cup-Winners' Cup honours. He captained City to their last major success, the 976 League Cup, and won 5 England caps. Doyle made 563 (7) appearances for City, scoring 41 oals. 1967/68 appearances: 37 (1). Goals: 5.

Manchester City's 1967/68 championship winning squad. From left to right, back row: Alan Oakes, Neil oung, George Heslop, Ken Mulhearn, Colin Bell, Glyn Pardoe, Mike Summerbee. Front row: Malcolm Allison, avid Connor, Francis Lee, Tony Book, Tony Coleman, Mick Doyle, Johnny Hart.

PLAYER AND MANAGEMENT PROFILES

George Heslop, centre half: Signed from Everton in September 1965 for £25,000, he went on to become one of the shrewdest purchases of the Mercer/Allison era. Impeccable throughout the Championship campaign, Heslop was superb in the air, adding solidity and power to the defence. He missed one game all season. Heslop will be remembered for scoring in the Manchester derby at Old Trafford, which City went on to win 3-1 in arguably their best performance of the season. During his City career Heslop won First Division, Second Division, League Cup and European Cup-Winners' Cup honours. He made 195 (3) appearances, scoring one goal. 1967/68 appearances: 41. Goals: 1.

Alan Oakes, wing half: Joined City as an amateur, making his League debut in 1959/60. Unassuming, consistent and devoted, Oakes gave incredible service over eighteen seasons. During the Championship season Tony Coleman and Neil Young in particular benefited from his penetrating passes. Oakes scored in a 6-0 thrashing of Leicester City and a draw at Sheffield United. During renowned City career, Oakes enjoyed First Division, Second Division, FA Cup, League Cup (2) and European Cup Winners' Cup successes. Top of the all-time appearances list, Oakes played a record 676 (4) games, scoring 34 goals. 1967/8 appearances: 41. Goals: 2.

Colin Bell, forward: Nicknamed 'Nijinsky' because of his non-stop running, incredible stamina and boundless enthusiasm, Bell is a City all-time great. Signed from Bury in March 1966, Bell made his debut for City aged seventeen. A consistent scorer throughout the Championship campaign, Bell notched crucial strikes against Leeds United and Manchester United and a brace in the penultimate game at Tottenham Hotspur. Bell won 48 England caps and enjoyed tremendous success at City, claiming First Division, FA Cup, League Cup and European Cup-Winners' Cup honours. Playing 498 (3) games, Bell is fifth on City's appearances list and third in the scoring charts with 153 goals, an amazing record curtailed by a serious knee injury in 1976 that forced him to eventually retire in 1979. 1967/68 appearances: 35. Goals: 14.

Francis Lee, forward: Signed from Bolton for £60,000 in October 1967, Lee soon became a favourite with fans. Made his debut in a victory against Wolves at Maine Road and scored his first goal the following week in an away win at Fulham. Lee was second top goalscorer with 16 goals, notching braces against Leicester City, West Ham and Stoke City, plus winning strikes against Sunderland and Burnley and the Blues' final goal in the title-clincher at Newcastle. Though not tall, his solid physique and bustling style made him a handful for defences; in addition a thundering shot brought him a stack of goals. An expert penalty taker, he struck a club record 15 in 1971/72. One of City's most prolific strikers, Lee enjoyed First Division, FA Cup, League Cup and European Cup-Winners' Cup successes. He later took over as club chairman, holding the position from 1994 to 1998. Making 328 (2) appearances, Lee scored 148 goals, including the Blues' winner in the 1970 European Cup Winners' Cup final. Lee also won 27 England caps and went on to gain another First Division title at Derby County. 1967/68 appearances: 31, Goals: 16.

Mike Summerbee, forward: Joe Mercer's first signing when he joined City in 1965. An orthodox outside right, Summerbee's presence, energy, aggression and pinpoint crossing created havoc for opposing defences. Summerbee missed only one match during the Championship campaign, playing central attacking role for all but the first three games. Summerbee struck 14 goals, including a brace Fulham and crucial goals in the final two games at Tottenham Hotspur and Newcastle United. ummerbee eventually assumed a more versatile role, sharing in many of the club's successes, earning rst Division, Second Division, FA Cup and League Cup winners' medals. Capped 8 times by England, ummerbee played 449 (3) matches, scoring 68 goals. 1967/68 appearances: 41. Goals: 14.

eil Young, forward: Signed professional forms at City in February 1961 and moved around the orward line until Joe Mercer switched him to inside left. The Blues' leading goalscorer during the hampionship season with a tally of 19, Young scored braces against Southampton, Leicester City, ulham, West Ham and, most memorably, in the title-clincher against Newcastle United. Young lways had time to spare and possessed excellent ball control and shooting power. Having also been pp scorer in City's Second Division Championship team, Young later won FA Cup and European Cup-Vinners' Cup honours too. Young made 413 (3) appearances for City, scoring 108 goals, the most mous being the Blues' winner in the 1969 FA Cup final. 1967/68 appearances: 40. Goals: 19.

ony Coleman, forward: Joined the Blues for £12,000 in March 1967 from Doncaster Rovers and uickly overcame his 'problem player' tag to become City's regular left-winger. Coleman's direct nd robust style created numerous chances for colleagues. During the Championship campaign oleman scored eight goals, including a brace against Burnley and City's second goal against verton in the final home game of the season. Coleman won First Division and FA Cup winner's nedals during four years at City. Coleman made 101 appearances, scoring 16 goals. 1967/68 ppearances: 38. Goals 8.

avid Connor, utility player: Joined City as an amateur in 1962. Connor was a key player during ity's promotion campaign in 1965/66 and went on to serve the club in every position except palkeeper and centre half. During the Blues' Championship season, Connor played in defence, nidfield and attack, scoring in City's draw at Everton. In twelve years at Maine Road, Connor gained rst Division, Second Division and FA Cup winner's medals. Connor made 152 (11) appearances, coring 10 goals. 1967/68 appearances: 8 (2). Goals: 1.

Iso played

aul Hince, appearances 6, goals 2

tan Horne, appearances 4

obby Kennedy, appearances 4 (2)

an Bowles, appearances 4, goals 2

oy Cheetham, appearances 2 (2)

hris Jones, appearances 2

lan Ogley, appearances 2

ohn Clay, appearances 1 (1)

hampionship season statistics are for First Division games only. International caps are career totals.

Other titles published by Tempus

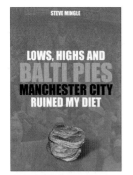

Lows, Highs and Balti Pies Manchester City Ruined my Diet
STEVE MINGLE

In this hilarious memoir, City fan Steve Mingle recounts his experiences of following the Blues through the good times and the bad. Infused with the humour for which the club's fans are renowned, it features his recollections of 100 matches, each of which, for better or worse, has become permanently lodged in his brain. Great games and great players; unbelievable cock-ups and stunning incompetence. They're all here, enhanced with a multitude of anecdotes, to provide a richly entertaining personal history of the club.

0 7524 3178 1

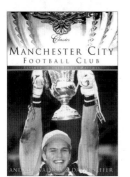

Manchester City FC Classics Seventy of the Finest Matches
ANDREW WALDON & DAVID SAFFER

Each of Manchester City's dedicated followers will have their own favourite match. This book traces the long history of the Blues through seventy unforgettable encounters over more than a century of highs and lows. Maine Road heroes like Francis Lee, Tommy Johnson and Niall Quinn all feature, as do personalities such as Joe Mercer, Joe Royle and Malcolm Allison.

0 7524 2255 3

Rugby League in Manchester
GRAHAM MORRIS

Over the past century, rugby league has had a strong presence in Manchester, with no fewer than eleven venues staging the sport within a four-mile radius of the city centre. With over 200 illustrations, this unique publication retraces the roots of Manchester's rugby league heritage and is a fascinating reminder of the many great moments and matches that have taken place there.

0 7524 3087 4

Lancashire CCC 100 Greats
KEITH HAYHURST

This book celebrates 100 of the best players to have represented Lancashire CCC since the club was formed in 1864. From the exceptional amateurs that dominated the team in the early years, through the heroes of the late 1960s that made Lancashire the kings of one-day cricket, to modern heroes such as Michael Atherton and Andrew Flintoff, this publication includes biographies, statistics and illustrations of Lancashire's finest.

0 7524 2405 X

If you are interested in purchasing other books published by Tempus, or in case you have difficulty finding any Tempus books in your local bookshop, you can also place orders directly through our website

www.tempus-publishing.com